ESSAYS IRREVERENT

Robert Warren Cromey

iUniverse, Inc.
Bloomington

Essays Irreverent

iUniverse books may be ordered through booksellers or by contacting:

iUniverse
1663 Liberty Drive
Bloomington, IN 47403
www.iuniverse.com
1-800-Authors (1-800-288-4677)

Because of the dynamic nature of the Internet, any web addresses or links contained in this book may have changed since publication and may no longer be valid. The views expressed in this work are solely those of the author and do not necessarily reflect the views of the publisher, and the publisher hereby disclaims any responsibility for them.

Any people depicted in stock imagery provided by Thinkstock are models, and such images are being used for illustrative purposes only.

Certain stock imagery © Thinkstock.

ISBN: 978-1-4759-4092-3 (sc)
ISBN: 978-1-4759-4093-0 (e)

Printed in the United States of America

iUniverse rev. date: 9/5/2012

CONTENTS

FOREWORD

Robert takes a liberal (some might say radical) view about most everything, as you will quickly learn when you read this book. He addresses a number subjects, and he doesn't censor himself. He is not rude or unkind (Well, maybe he does poke the Republican party a time or two), but he is fearless. One of the many things I love about Robert is his complete honesty. I don't always agree with him, and that's just fine with him.

Robert came into my life over a decade ago when I wandered into Trinity Church, San Francisco, where he was the rector. I went to check out his Bible study group, because the Bible as literature interested me. I didn't hold out much hope that a church study group would take a literary approach, but I thought I give it a try. A few minutes after Robert began to speak I knew immediately I had come to the right place. In fact, I stayed for the church service, which I certainly hadn't plan to do.

I learned much from Robert during those sessions. We discussed the Bible as folk history, poetry, stories, and inspiration. He explained its history—who wrote what, when, and why—which helped me understand the book in a new and helpful light. He also pointed out how it held wisdom that could be applied to contemporary life. Through Robert I came to understand I didn't have to be a sheep; I could doubt and question away. He spoke of his views but he encouraged everyone to find their own paths, their own way of relating to the church, the Bible and religion.

Soon I surprised myself by becoming an official member of the congregation. I attended services fairly regularly and took part in other activities Trinity offered. These activities gave me the opportunity to get to know Robert and his charming wife, Ann.

Later, after he retired, we became friends and met for lunch from time to time. I felt flattered when he asked me to be his writing buddy, which means we check in almost daily through email, if only a line or two, to report what writing we have accomplished. Doing this encourages regular writing. Certainly, on an off day, I sometimes make myself write, because I don't want to have to tell Robert I didn't. Being writing buddies has deepened our friendship over the years.

Robert has so enriched my life in many, many ways. He remains a great and good influence on me. I could write much more about Robert, but this is his book. So I will close by saying thank you, Robert, for everything. I treasure out friendship.

Michelle Schmidt
San Francisco
July 2012

PREFACE

I put these writings together so that many of my most important ideas may be found in one place. Family, friends and colleagues may find some of them helpful, useful, informative, educational, controversial, challenging or stupid.

When I retired in 2001, I set a goal for myself of writing 500 words a day. I was used to writing sermons, articles, letters and emails during my days, weeks and years as a parish priest and the decade I was a therapist. Writing seems a good way to keep my mind active and challenged. Somewhere I thought is might help ward off dementia and Alzheimer's. We'll see if that works.

I set out to write a memoir, *RWC Memoir*, which I self-published in 2009, then *So You Want to Get Married* in 2010, I think. Lulu.com is the place where they can be ordered. In 1992 Alamo Square Press published *In God's Image, Lesbian and Gay Rights in the Eyes of the Church*. It is now out of print, but Amazon.com seems to be able to find stuff.

A few of these essays may also be found in *RWC Memoir*. My views on pornography, drugs and prostitution will always be relevant, as our society can never take a humane attitude to people who choose to play in those arenas. Sumptuary laws, in which people and governments attempt to control people's personal behaviors, are always with us and failing.

There is a substantial section on sermons and preaching. I had a long career as a preacher. I mentored preachers in the College of Preachers, in Washington, D.C., in 1967, and seminarians and associates in parishes where I was rector. I have read lots of books about preaching. Since I retired, I have listened to many sermons and been so often disappointed in the lack of inspiration, social action and relevance from pulpits. Preachers seem too full of Bible, theology and spirituality to connect to the daily lives of their listeners. I hope this section will help clergy and lay people prepare and listen more deeply when the word of God is presented. Clergy seldom discuss their sermons either beforehand or after delivery. Lay people seldom give feedback of any depth. Perhaps they are afraid of offending the preacher or do not feel competent to do so. Perhaps some discussion of my ideas in the essays will stimulate discussion.

I know some will say that this collection is again a Cromey ego trip and bid for publicity. Such statements are quite true. My good sense of myself and my confidence in my ideas make it easy to write and speak what I choose and take the consequences. It is also true that I love publicity. I enjoy seeing my name in the paper and puss on television sometimes--not often enough, actually.

Finally, I want to thank Michelle Schmidt for her encouragement and support. All problems or errors are my responsibility, however.

Robert Warren Cromey
San Francisco
July 2012

ACKNOWLEDGEMENTS

This book is dedicated to my wife Elizabeth Ann Cromey and to my daughters Leigh Cromey, Sarah Buck and Jessica Buck.

MARRIAGE

A couple wrote me a note after I led a pre-marital seminar with them recently. They walked away from our time together with a new sense of *mindfulness* about their relationship and forthcoming marriage. Their response is exactly what I want to my pre-marital counseling.

The Mystery of Relationships

Why two people meet and fall in love is a mystery. There are so many nice, attractive people out there, yet two people find each other and develop that special juice that links them and allows them to make a choice to be with each other. A mystery indeed.

The Dance of Close Yet Free[1]

We can be close and intimate with our partner yet free to be ourselves and enjoy other interests that our partner may not share. *He* likes to watch football on television; *she* cares little for sports. *She* wants a night off each week to be with women friends; *he* wants to hang out with his old cronies. *She* loves the out doors and hiking; *he* wants to play golf or basketball. None of these activities is bad or wrong, but often these interests create conflict, especially with the newly married. Real intimacy

---

1 *Close Yet Free* is an idea I got from Gerald Walker Smith, a Bay Area therapist and consultant and good friend.

cannot be maintained unless people have freedom as well as closeness.

These conflicts can be negotiated and agreements made and kept. Let's start with a man watching football or any sport on television. These events are scheduled in advanced; you can predict times when the games will be played and approximately how long they will take. His partner can see this as free time to pursue other interests. I know a man who wants his wife to watch sports with him. *She* agrees to watch for a half hour, then goes on to do other things. A couple should make an agreement about what activities they will do separately and which ones together. These agreements can be renegotiated as needed.

Full Free Consent

For a marriage to work, the relationship must be entered into with full, free consent on the parts of both people. If a man is forced to marry a woman because she is pregnant by him and her father has a shotgun against his head to make sure the marriage takes place, that is not full, free consent on his part. If a woman has had a child or an abortion and has not told the intended groom, he does not have all the facts about her; he does not have full free consent.

I think each man and woman should have a full, frank discussion of the sexual experiences they have had with others. Who, what, when, where, how many, and what did you do? (Intercourse—oral and anal—mutual masturbation, names and so on.) These will be scary and threatening at first but can later become fun and of interest to the marital relationship. (Remember, these are not requirements, just suggestions about how to deepen and challenge a new relationship.)

If the man has been convicted of a crime and has spent time in prison, the woman cannot enter into marriage without all the facts about him. I read recently where a man was an illegal alien, did not tell his fiancé, and is now facing deportation. She could not have given full, free consent, because she did not have all the facts about him.

I'd like to take this a step or two further. The man and woman should know exactly how much money and how much debt each has. Money is often troublesome in marriages. A good start occurs before the marriage when each person is clear about his or her financial situation. Pre-nuptial agreements are popular now so that the whole financial picture of each is discussed and known beforehand.

How to be Faithful

When you make a vow to be faithful to one another, of course you intend to keep it. You intend to be with your spouse and with no one else for the rest of your life. At this time you cannot really imagine having sex with another person. But you may have jobs that take you traveling, you will meet attractive and interesting people in your work, classes, sporting events, church and just hanging out. It will be virtually impossible for you not to have sexual feelings from time to time toward people you meet. In fact the more you enjoy sex with your partner, the more sexual you will feel and be vulnerable to those feelings when you meet a person who excites you.

There is nothing wrong with those sexual feelings toward others. There is no sense in denying that the feelings exist. They are natural and normal in all people. In fact, denying them may even intensify them and make them more difficult to control. This is especially true if you meet someone who expresses sexual feelings toward you.

So what do you do? How do you control those delicious feelings, those dangerous and delightful feelings? You share them with your spouse. You tell him what you feel, whom you feel that way about and when it happens. You tell him what the person looks like and where have you seen him? You ask your spouse to understand the feelings. You promise him not to act on those feelings.

Now is the time, before you are married, to make an agreement with each other that it is okay to talk with each other about those sexual feelings toward others. Some people say they don't want to hear about their partners' sexual feelings toward others. That unwillingness may really get in the way of keeping your vow to be faithful to each other. Here is a situation where you have given your partner permission to have a secret, to withhold something from your relationship. You put your energy into withholding and keeping a secret that should be going into the relationship.

Grace

Religious people have the idea of grace; we call it God's gift to all people. To define it further, *grace* is the knowledge that all we have and all we are is an unearned gift. We do not earn our life, our parents, our eyes, our hands, our feet, our siblings. Yes, we work hard to earn our money. Many people work very hard and get little money. People who invest earn lots of money by doing nothing. I owned a building in San Francisco, held it for three years, did nothing to it and sold it for twice the price. That money was a grace, a free gift.

The person whom you are about to marry is a free gift to you. You did nothing to earn that gift. It is a mystery. When you look at this person, see him or her as a gift rather than someone you earned and who owes you something.

Sickness and Health

One of the vows you make to each other when you marry is to be with that person in sickness and health. When young people marry, it is hard to imagine their partners as sick. But think about your parents and grandparents, they probably had to take care of each other sometime when the other has been sick.

In a newspaper article about amputees just back from Iraq, there was a touching picture of a soldier lying in a big bed with the bare stumps of both legs peering out from his shorts. His lovely, blond wife lay next to him, smiling and chatting. His two young boys played at the foot of the bed. This couple now really knows what *in sickness and health* really mean. The article also reported that another wife with four young children took one look at her maimed, amputee husband and fled.

Most will not have to face such extremes; nevertheless, you agree to care for each other in those times of weakness and vulnerability. But look at this profound idea of partnership and its implication for deep physical and personal caring.

Ask for What You Want

You probably won't get what you want unless you ask for it. Your partner is not obliged to read your mind to discover what you want. "You should know what I want" is a deadly statement that expresses anger and puts responsibility in the hands of the other person. It is a way of not taking responsibility for oneself.

You are entitled to ask for what you want, anything at all. You are not entitled to get it. I am entitled to ask my wife to buy me a yacht. I am not entitled to get it. You are entitled to ask for sex every night, breakfast in bed and a massage every eight hours. There is nothing wrong with asking; you may even get many of the things you want.

People put a lot of energy into not asking or not finding the right time, the right mood or circumstance. If there is something you want or need, ask for it. It releases tension and anxiety. Ask for what you want, and you will clear the air, put the cards on the table and be ready for a discussion. Even if you don't get what you want, you will feel better just by having asked.

Try this. Each of you makes a list of all the things you really want—for the house, about vacations, how to treat in-laws, and so on. From this list agree on the things you can accept together and drop the ones that don't seem important. You will feel better for just getting out the wishes and desires you have or think you have.

Thank Each Other All the Time

All of us can never be thanked enough for what we do for our partners. Our partners can never be thanked enough for what they do for us. Make a list of all the things you are thankful for in your relationship. Be sure to include sex, cooking, cleaning, caring for the money, relationships with in-laws, appearance, dress, cleanliness, hairstyle, clothes, smell, kisses, touches. Keep thanking each other all the time. It will never be enough.

Strokes

In *The Marriage Journey* by Glover and Genzer, the authors write "…a healthy relationship needs twenty strokes for any negative. That's twenty hugs, kisses, compliments, smiles, winks, cuddles, little favors, affirmations, affectionate glances, private nicknames, 'I love yous,' jokes, thank-yous, attentive listenings, nips on the back of the neck, back rubs, steamy showers, heartfelts 'you're wonderfuls….' "

If you are giving and receiving these strokes regularly and with meaning, negative remarks and arguments can be handled with grace and ease. If there is a deep well of affection, thanks and praise in a relationship, arguments can be handled with love and support for each other.

Lots of Sex

Sexual activity depends on the drives and needs of each individual in the relationship. One person may have more desire for sex than the other. Individual differences should be honored. Like everything else, these needs and desires must be talked about openly and honestly. Frank and specific behaviors can be scary, then informative and even fun. There is a big part of sex that is funny, clumsy, awkward and still deeply powerful.

Sex is the glue that holds many couples together. It is a natural and normal for people to be touching, penetrating and savoring each other's bodies on a regular basis. Many people say they don't want a lot of sex. I like the maxim, "The more you get, the more you want." Really close and intimate sex draws us closer to our partners. Intimacy is maintained by having intimate physical sex and intimate sharing conversations and communications. These two go together. Those after-sex chats, lying in bed recovering from orgasms, can be the most intimate and open conversations a couple can have. Good sex makes for good marriages.

"I Love You" Five Times a Day

Like thanking, you cannot be told enough that your partner loves you. Your partner can never get enough of being told that you love him or her. It may sound repetitious and trite but try it anyway. Tell your partner, "I love you" at least five times a day.

Forgiveness

You will have fights, arguments and disagreements. You will hurt each other, be sad and angry, then after a while will want to kiss and make up. Here is a little formula that may help the process.

1. Admit what you have done.
2. Do what you can to make it right.
3. Do what you can not to repeat the behavior.
4. Ask for and accept forgiveness.

In this process you will feel healed and whole again. You will feel and be forgiven.

No More Faithful Monogamy

When I do premarital counseling with people, I discover they do not know the difference between fidelity and monogamy. They think they are the same thing. In my Webster's New Collegiate Dictionary, *monogamy* means, in an archaic sense, the practice of marrying only once in a lifetime. In the present day it means the custom of being married to one person at a time. Fidelity means steadfast in affection or, in the case of marriage, to forsake all others. So one can be monogamous and not faithful. I know of couples that clearly plan to stay together but have other sexual relationships. These are rare. We do get awfully jealous when we know our spouse is having sex with another person.

Life-long, faithful monogamy is on the way out. Many Christians already practice polygamy with successive partners. It is called marriage after divorce. Robert Wright, an evolutionary psychologist, suggests infidelity is in the genes of some percentage of the population. "The good news is that human beings are designed to fall in love. The bad news is that they aren't designed to stay there. It is 'natural' for both men and women at some times and under certain circumstances to suddenly find a spouse unattractive, irritating, wholly unreasonable."

Natural does not mean unchangeable. The human mind is flexible enough to shape our behavior. But, when we know there are hundreds of millions of people on planet earth, there will be many people who are not going to commit to a life-long, faithful partnership. Why make this demand?

Church and society believe children thrive best in stable families. They are healthier than children from broken homes. The family is the basic unit of society; anything that weakens it destroys the fabric of that society. Stable families produce happier and less violent children than those from divorced families. Let's assume all that is true, yet one half of marriages in our country end in divorce.

Religious bodies cling to the notion of faithful monogamy. They hold it up as the highest ideal for all, especially all their members. Religious groups proclaim the dignity of faithful, monogamous marriages. Many even allow for divorce and re-marriage. However, they fail to provide pastoral teaching and assistance to people who cannot and do not stay faithful, who commit adultery or just need to move on to other relationships.

Suppose people did not have the weight of the vow to a life-long, faithful monogamous commitment. Suppose we didn't make the breakup of a family a moral disaster. Suppose we in fact prepared people for divorce in the way we prepare them for marriage.

I see a day coming when we will perform marriages between people omitting the promise to forsake all others and to be faithful as long as you both shall live. The church could give the couple the option of not having to promise to be faithful and monogamous. Leave it up to the couple to decide what they are going to do about the future of their marriage. We can prepare young people for the fact that they have only a fifty-fifty chance of keeping their vows. We can teach that relationships change—for better and sometimes for worse.

It is much more common for couples to have extra-marital affairs but stay married. They do not discuss this with their partners. The price they pay is a lack of honesty and deep intimacy. By not sharing with one's spouse this important, emotionally laden other relationship, they withhold basic energy from their primary relationship. These relationships usually lack real, personal intimacy.

I am in a faithful, monogamous relationship. I am wildly jealous at the thought of my wife having sex with another man. In an earlier marriage, I had relationships with other women outside of my marriage. I kept them secret. While the affairs were delicious and delightful, they adulterated and ruined my first marriage. It caused pain and hardship for my first wife, my children and ultimately for myself.

When I first married in 1952, I was totally unprepared for my desire and attraction to other women. My clear intention was for life-long, faithful monogamy. I was a virgin when I married. After several years of marriage I wanted to know how other women looked when naked and how they felt sexually. I had a lot of sexual drive and energy. My wife and I made love three times a week at least. She had more than a full-time job looking after our children and home. She could not possibly keep up with my sexual demands and needs. I was embarrassed to let her know how much sex I wanted. I never discussed it with her.

My own experience and observations of the hundreds of couples I have counseled convinces me there is something built into the character of many men and women that makes them want more than one mate.

My present wife and I were both divorced. Each of us had sexual experience with others before we married. Our vows of faithful monogamy are based on knowing the pains and sorrows of failed marriages. We knew the misery of jealousy. We were experienced, mature adults making a decision to be faithful and monogamous.

High monogamy is a term popularized by writer George Leonard. It means "a long-term relationship in which both members are voluntarily committed to erotic exclusivity, not because of legal, moral or religious scruples, not because of timidity and inertia, but because they seek challenge and adventure." My wife and I subscribe to that ideal, but I am convinced it comes after a lot of relationships, trial and error and learning from the past. The church offers little or no help to couples wishing to practice high monogamy.

Perhaps one good thing about young people having a number of sexual partners before they marry is that they are less apt to be intrigued by sex with a partner outside of marriage.

I look at the beautiful, young people eager for marriage who come to Trinity to be married. All are living together; none are virgins. I hope they can keep their vows, but there is a fifty-fifty chance they won't. They are not prepared to face their attraction to others. They will be shocked by the weariness and boredom of some relationships. It will be hard to face mercurial sex drives that seemed so stable in the early days of their marriage.

There are some communication skills to help committed couples prepare for their natural attraction to others. I use them in premarital counseling. I tell couples to be really open and honest with each other when they are sexually attracted to someone at the office, school or gym. If a woman is turned on by a colleague, then she should come home and tell her spouse about how she felt and who the person is. If the man dreams of having sex with a woman at work, he should tell his wife about it immediately. When either one fantasizes about sex with another, talk about it with their partner. I urge couples to make these fantasies part of their basic relationship. This does take trust and openness, but this sharing of dreams and feelings will blow up the sexual charge directed toward another person. It brings that sexual energy back into the basic relationship.

But when most relationships have poor communication to begin with, it is hard to share such dangerous material with a spouse. Sports, money, kids and relatives are the basic topics of communication in most marriages. Talking about sexual fantasies with another will be hard to endure.

The major Christian denominations meet regularly proclaiming the centrality of faithful, monogamous marriage for Christian people. These churches might lurch into the twenty-first century by looking at the absurdity of demanding faithful monogamy as a basis for marriage. Churches should be preparing people getting married to face the fifty-percent divorce rate and help them either achieve good marriages or get dignified divorces and pursue opportunities for another marriage in the church.

Viagra

What a blessing to have a stiff, hard cock when Ann and I make love. It reminds me of my teenage years, when I thought I had a perpetual hard on. I used to be so embarrassed when I got hard. I thought the whole world was watching my damp crotch. I tried to hide it by sitting down, carrying my books in front of my body or doing something that would make people look elsewhere. I loved the feelings of my erect penis, and I hated the idea that someone might notice that I had one. Other boys didn't ever seem to have erections; I never noticed any one else with one. In fact I never even noticed anyone noticing mine.

Then, after I masturbated for the first time in Brooklyn, I loved touching my cock and enjoying the sexual feelings so very much. Then I masturbated a lot. In high school I was embarrassed by the locker room jokes about cocks and though it beneath me to enter in to such joking. Then when I went to dances, I was happy and embarrassed by my erections, and it was never mentioned by any of the girls with whom I danced. Maybe they didn't notice. Maybe it is just in books that girls say they felt boys' cocks harden when they danced.

As time rolled on and I was married to Lillian in 1952, we had lots of good sex, making a quick and easy satisfying sexual adjustment. Three children were conceived, and we settled into sex three times a week all during that marriage. My cock performed admirably with other women throughout my divorced years—the eleven years I was a bachelor and had many women as lovers.

Ann and I have had a splendid and active hot sex life. At first we had sex three times a day then every day at least once for many years. As I got older, it was a combination of intercourse and blow jobs. My penis did not get erect so quickly and for a while I couldn't maintain an erection very long after entering Ann.

In the early days I worried that I would come too soon. That happened from time to time, but after a while I had plenty of staying power. Then in my sixties, it wasn't that I came too soon; it was that my penis softened, and I didn't come at all. Ann would blow me to an orgasm, and that made me feel good; she seemed most happy to help. She loves sex and enjoys all its playful variations.

When Viagra came along, I was given some for my seventieth birthday. Ann was reluctant to have me use it, because she was afraid I would become addicted. I used it from time to time. I took 25 mg, and it produced good erection the first day that lasted into a day or two later.

In my seventy-fifth year, 2005-06, I began to use it every time we had sex, and that has been wonderful. I would like to go back to having sex every day, but Ann has some menopausal vaginal delicacies that such regular sex causes her some pain. So we have sex three times a week at least, and it is quite wonderful. My orgasms are strong, and Ann seems to enjoy herself too.

The first Viagra I ever got was from a doctor acquaintance who gave me twenty-five 25 mg pills. My ontologist, Maury Mink, generously gave me a bunch of samples. So I had quite a supply. When we were in Paris in 2004, I bought some there, because I was running out and one doesn't need a prescription to purchase them in France. To make them go further I cut them in half and that worked quite nicely. Later, I got Gary Feldman, my internist, to prescribe more. He gave me 100 mgs, and I cut them in quarters, which worked quite nicely. What a true blessing for us older men—and women too—to have an erect penis within a half-hour—the pill takes at least that long to activate. I love the old cliché, "Better living through chemistry."

RELIGION

Ambiguity

An old and dear friend of mine is now very conservative. Once he was a strong supporter of civil rights for African-Americans. He and his wife adopted a black child and brought her into their home. A strong supporter of lesbian, gay, bisexual, and transgender (LGBT) rights, he gave money to support that movement. We lost close touch for many years. We began to be in touch more when email became more popular. We grew adept in communicating that way. I was quite shocked that he had voted for the Bushes and Republicans since before Reagan. I didn't think much of it since my brother also voted for Reagan—and I assume Republican ever since those days. We get along fine but don't talk much about politics.

But I noticed my old friend, let's call him Liam, had become shrill. Obama will ruin the country. Health Care Reform will ruin the economy. All Muslims are bent on ruining democracy. This trend has become more noticeable as Liam seems out to try to convince me to change my positions on issues and to get my support for his view of things. On the issue of the Muslim takeover there is a touch of hysteria and paranoia.

He has a lot of support for this kind of thinking. Right-wing talk shows; the Tea Party Movement; and apocalyptic, end-of-the-world fears abound in the United States. Liam may be fired up by that support and now conventional thinking. But I do wonder if there is something of a more psychological anxiety in him. However, I am not his therapist. He has not asked me for help, and I cannot diagnose him.

Thinking about this change in Liam, I also wonder if he, like many people, has a hard time with ambiguity, the ability to hold comfortably two divergent views at the same time. I think that ability is a definition of a mature person. Fully developed, authentic persons look clearly at what they believe, hold to that belief and are understanding and sympathetic to other people's quite divergent points of view.

Many people wholeheartedly support the right of Israel to exist. They just as strongly hold the view that the Israeli government's treatment of the Palestinians is unjust and cruel. One can fully support President Obama's presidency and be completely against his policies in Afghanistan and Iraq. One can be a full-fledged, people-oriented Democrat and understand and disagree with the Republican business-and-economic-centered point of view.

This doesn't mean that one doesn't take a strong stand on issues. Taking a strong stand does not mean dishonoring or holding in contempt the views of others. There are times when one must take a stand and make sure that those who disagree are not hurting others.

In a strike against a coalmine company, one can understand the need of workers for more pay and more safety. The owners have to earn enough money to run the company. Seeing both sides does not prevent one from taking a position. One must judge who is being hurt most. Where is injustice? Which is the weaker party in the weakest position? I tend to be on the side of the weaker and the underdog, but I can see and disagree with others who take the opposing side.

As a strong advocate for civil rights for all in the 1960s, I could see that many of my fellow Episcopalians were hurt by my taking a strong stand for blacks, gays and lesbians. I had to decide which side I was on. The minorities would be hurt if I did not support them. My middle-class, white co-religionists would be hurt if I supported the minorities. It was not a hard choice really. As a follower of Jesus, I chose the side of the weak, the poor and the outcast.

My friend Liam supported the minorities in the '60s, and maybe he still does, but I hope he can appreciate and understand the other side of issues and the people that support those issues. Life would be easier if the world was good or bad, black or white, right or wrong. But it isn't. We are presented a world with shades of gray, which is another way of seeing the world of moral, ethical and political choice as ambiguous.

Christian Republicans?

Here are basic principles of the Republican Party.[2]

> Republicans emphasize the role of free markets and individual achievement as the primary factors behind economic prosperity. To this end, they favor laissez-faire economics, fiscal conservatism, and the promotion of personal responsibility over welfare programs...."

> ...They believe private spending is usually more efficient than government spending. Republicans oppose the estate tax...

> The party opposes a government-run single-payer health care system, believing such a system constitutes socialized medicine and is in favor of a personal or employer-based system of insurance, supplemented by Medicare for the elderly and Medicaid, which covers approximately 40% of the poor. The GOP has a mixed record of supporting the historically popular Social Security, Medicare and Medicaid programs...

---

2 http://en.wikipedia.org/wiki/Republican_Party_%28United_States%29#Economic_policies

Republicans are generally opposed by labor union management and members, and have supported various legislation on the state and federal levels, including right to work legislation and the Taft-Hartley Act, which gives workers the right not to participate in unions, as opposed to a closed shop, which prohibits workers from choosing not to join unions in workplaces. Some Republicans are opposed to increases in the minimum wage, believing that such increases hurt many businesses by forcing them to cut jobs and services, export jobs overseas, and raise the prices of goods to compensate for the decrease in profit.

Can you be a Christian and be a Republican? The Party officially opposes health care for all, welfare programs and programs to provide homes for the homeless. Champions of capitalism, Republicans are blind to the fact that laissez-faire capitalism leaves a tremendous wake of poor and hungry people in its desire to make money for corporations and individuals.

One Republican suburban housewife told me she didn't want to hear another word about the homeless. Another good friend told me that we can give to charity, "not touch the capitalistic system and pray for those sadly left behind." Another Republican told me that the poor already have medical insurance. They can go to emergency rooms. I suggested ER's don't give tests for eyeglasses or glaucoma.

Republicans are against labor unions, as they are seen as interfering with laissez-faire capitalism. Labor unions, however, are one of the means by which poor people can get together and bargain for better wages and safer working conditions. Republicans scoff at the government Office for Safety and Health Administration (OSHA) feeling this is government interfering with the free flow of business. The fact that OSHA protects the health and safety of working people is overlooked.

The capitalistic system must not be tampered with. Some believe when the rich get truly rich and the economy flourishes money will trickle down to the poor and homeless. Experience teaches us that it does not work. Most have made their bundle and do not want to look back or care for those whom they have never met. Few Republicans work in slum neighborhoods, visit the permanently maimed soldiers living out their days in institutions or represent farm laborers fighting injustices foisted on them by greedy farmers.

Churches are full of Republicans. They are generous supporters of churches. Many clergy are members of the Grand Old Party. They are comfortable with the rich and the upwardly mobile—in fact their salaries depend on the good will of many Republicans. Republicans give generously to universities, charities, foundations and churches. Much urban Republicans' social lives depend on high-ticket social and artistic balls, galas and dinners, which give the leftovers from the expenses of the event to eagerly awaiting charities, including churches. Republicans and many of the rich want to choose where their money goes. They want to control how to do good and what the good causes are. That is natural of course.

Republicans and others enjoy the institutional church. They enjoy the traditions, music, and a feel-good experience on a Sunday morning. They do not like sermons that talk about politics or the events of the world. They want a comfortable, warm friendly place to sing the hymns and to enjoy good choir music. Both the Presbyterian and Episcopal Churches have been called the Republican Party at prayer. Mormons are the new winners in that category.

One of the reasons congregations of the mainline churches— such as like Presbyterian, Episcopal, Methodist and Lutheran— are declining in numbers is because well-off people do hear the gospel of Jesus emphasizing care for the poor and equal rights for minorities. They hear this in the readings from the Bible. This challenge to their conservative values makes them want to leave the comfortable pew to which they have become accustomed. Few preachers dare preach very specifically about the relationship between Biblical teachings and the values of the Republican Party. The other reason they leave is that the sermons and liturgies are so boring.

Now I want to talk about what it means to be a follower of Jesus as opposed to being a member of the institution called *church*. Jesus' focus is on the weakest of all people— children, sick, insane, handicapped, bereaved and the poor and the hungry. A political party that believes in personal responsibility neglecting the weakest to go it alone cannot be in any way conceived of as Christian. Millions of people in Africa cannot take personal responsibility or go it alone when all they have are the beggars' remains from capitalistic, free enterprise enriching corrupt politicians.

Followers of Jesus believe in feeding the hungry; providing hospitality to those with no homes; and healing the lame, blind and diseased. Christians see these values as the core of following Jesus, whose vision of God's kingdom was a perfect place where all would be fed and peace would reign. Christians believe, because that kingdom has not come, it is our job to work toward relieving suffering, poverty, hunger and striving for peace in the broken world we live in now.

Blessed *are* the poor in spirit: for theirs is the kingdom of heaven.

> *Jesus said unto him, If thou wilt be perfect, go and sell that thou hast, and give to the poor, and thou shalt have treasure in heaven: and come and follow me.*

> Mathew 5:3, 19:21

> *The Spirit of the Lord is upon me, because he hath anointed me to preach the gospel to the poor; he hath sent me to heal the brokenhearted, to preach deliverance to the captives, and recovering of sight to the blind, to set at liberty them that are bruised,*

> *But I say to you that listen, Love your enemies, do good to those who hate you. bless those who curse you, pray for those who abuse you.29 If anyone strikes you on the cheek, offer the other also; and from anyone who takes away your coat do not withhold even your shirt. 30Give to everyone who begs from*

you; and if anyone takes away your goods, do not ask for them again. 31Do to others as you would have them do to you.

Luke 4:18, 27

Jesus saith unto him, I say not unto thee, Until seven times: but, Until seventy times seven.

Matthew 18:22

These values jostle the heart not only of Republican values but those of the accommodating and institutional church as well.

The followers of Jesus pray with their feet in marches and vigils for peace and justice. In the small, conservative town of Andover, Massachusetts, a group of people, some Christians, stand every night, winter and summer, in a vigil for peace and justice. Traditional church people pray and worship well but are often deaf to what the *New Testament* teaches about the rich, problems of worshiping money and the plight of the poor and sick. I heard a sermon recently in which the preacher said that Jesus was not really against the rich. He went on to say how many rich people in his church were doing good in the community. I'd call it putting band-aids on gushing wounds. He never once suggested the rich could change the rules and laws that keep the rich richer and the poor poorer. I guess we know who pays his salary.

Should the radical followers of Jesus leave the church and found another? No; such a group would soon become an institution. Followers of Jesus remain in the church, do their work, and pressure the institution to be more fully followers of Jesus rather than reflecting the values of conventional society.

Should Republicans leave the church? No. The church needs their money. (I am a beneficiary of the Church Pension Fund, a very wealthy and conservative fund probably managed by Republican and conservative business people since its founding by J.P. Morgan.) The followers of Jesus can still keep working on them to follow Jesus more radically. We can do this best if they are in the church.

One teacher puts it this way.

The majority perspective in church and society assumes that by wealth power, organization or hard work we can get things to turn out the way we want.... A minority perspective seeks to embody and witness to the way of Jesus, but without embracing worldly power, wealth or influence. A minority church uses imagination and learns to survive over the long haul.

Republicans are good and decent people, but the party to which they belong comes nowhere near reflecting the work of Jesus in the world. The party platform, goals and purposes are antithetical to the heart of the gospel of Jesus. Republican church members should be clear that their party and the teachings of Jesus are in radical opposition to each other.

My soul doth magnify the Lord....
He hath put down the mighty from their seat
And hath exalted the humble and meek.

He hath filled the hungry with good things
And the rich he hath sent empty away.

Luke 1

Clergy Taking a Stand

Clergy often fear involvement in social and political actions for justice—such as participating in vigils, demonstrations, picket lines, protests, media conferences, signing petitions or writing letters to the editor. Clergy values usually support the ends of such events like peace, racial equality; lesbian, gay, bisexual, transvestite (LGBT) rights; unions and workers. Some rightly fear their congregations or superiors, such as Bishops and judicatory supervisors, will criticize them. Some fear they will be passed over for promotions, better jobs and bigger ministries. Some fear losing their jobs and fear they will have trouble supporting their families and themselves. People are different. Some are more aggressive than others; some are more willing to take risks. Is it in their nature?

It is true that outspoken liberal and radical clergy seldom get elected bishops or become deans of cathedrals or posh parishes. Clerics who speak out do not make good committee members or patient planners or negotiators, but many liberal, radical clergy have done very well in churches and as teachers.

James A. Pike was elected Bishop of California in 1958 after publicly espousing what were very hot issues in those days: birth control, abortion rights, civil rights for African-Americans and a liberal theology. He was featured on radio and television during the very conservative 1950s.

Malcolm Boyd was a freedom rider to the South in the 1960s and gained national attention as an activist on social and political issues, especially full freedom for African-Americans. He made a career of writing, speaking and performing on college campuses and nightclubs. He assisted in parishes in Los Angeles.

John Spong had solid liberal credentials on all issues and was elected Bishop of Newark in the 1970s.

In the early 1960s a group of clergy founded and supported San Francisco's Council on Religion and the Homosexual, an organization of clergy and lay people, to study and understand the homosexual community, which was being harassed and persecuted in the City and Bay Area.

On January 1, 1965, hundreds of gays and lesbians attended a New Year's Ball, a fundraiser for the Council on Religion and the Homosexual (CRH). Police invaded this private benefit event. They took flash photographs of partygoers in a blatant attempt at intimidating the guests as they entered California Hall on Polk Street to go to the ballroom. One woman and three lawyers were arrested for blocking the police from entering, and two men were arrested for alleged lewd conduct. The ball continued without further interference.

When the San Francisco Police Department had heard about the ball, it attempted to force the rented hall's owners to cancel the event. Some of the leaders of the Council, I among them, had met with the police to explain the purposes of the Council and the Ball with the idea of heading off any trouble. The police were more interested in the theology of the clergy and, noticing wedding rings, asked if our wives knew of this event. After more discussion, we left the meeting feeling sure the ball would go on without interruption.

When police demanded entry into the hall, three CRH lawyers explained to them that under California law, the event was a private party and they could not enter unless they bought tickets. The lawyers were then arrested, as was a ticket-taker, on charges of obstructing an officer.

On January 3, 1965, seven clergy, who were among the founders and supporters of CRH, held a press conference ripping the police for their invasion of the private party.

Those participating in the press conference were the late Reverend Lewis Durham, program director of the Glide Foundation; the Reverend Robert Warren Cromey of the Episcopal Diocese of California; the Reverend Cecil Williams, Director of Glide's Church and Community Ministry; the Reverend Fred Bird, pastor of St. Johns Methodist Church; the Reverend Charles Lewis of the North Beach Lutheran Ministry; the late Reverend Dr. Clarence Caldwell, of the United Methodist Church and the Reverend Ted McIlvenna of the Glide Foundation.

There was a lot of media coverage after the conference on radio, television and in newspapers. Further articles and pictures of the clergy appeared. One person said, "Well, that's the end of your career in the church." Not so.

Here is what happened to the clergy involved in that controversial action and media conference.

- Lewis Durham served the Glide Foundation and National Sex Forum until his death.
- Cecil Williams had been in protests and arrested numerous times supporting the poor and the elderly. He served as pastor of Glide Memorial Methodist Church in San Francisco where he raised millions

of dollars for the church's ministry to the poor and disenfranchised.

- Robert Warren Cromey had a private practice as a Marriage and Family Therapist and served as Rector of Trinity, San Francisco, for twenty years before retiring in 2002.
- Fred Bird went into academics after moving from the Bay Area to Canada.
- Charles Lewis became San Franicsco's Night Minister for many years.
- Clarence Caldwell served the United Methodist Church, then became a Marriage and Family Therapist until his death.
- Ted McIlvenna left the active ministry of the United Methodist Church and founded the Institute for the Advanced Study of Human Sexuality in San Francisco where he worked until his retirement.

Taking a stand does not mean loss of income or employment. Taking a stand on important issues in fact gives clergy credibility and stature. In some denominations clergy lead large and growing churches by taking a stand against LGBT people and against abortion. They take a stand, all right, but not one liberal and radical care to espouse. Some churches, such as Glide; Trinity San Francisco, and All Saints, Pasadena, flourished when they became noted for specific ministries and activities of a liberal bent.

Not taking a stand means many churches remain small, lack excitement and seem uncertain where they are going and what they are trying to do in the society. We all want to preach the gospel of Jesus. Many offer spirituality and deepening worship, but that is not enough. Making the spirituality a specific reality is what makes a church vibrant.

- How many youth groups teach kids about peace and show how to become conscientious objectors?

- How many parishes regularly invite LGBT people to come to classes to share their stories? How about creating dialogues with African-Americans, AA members, Muslims or Asians?
- How many parishes adopt a veteran's hospital and visit soldiers who have lost their limbs, their sight or their minds? Most of them will be in hospitals for the rest of their lives.
- I saw a photo of St. Francis Lutheran Church members in the newspaper walking together in the AIDS walk. How many churches walk en masse in the annual breast cancer fund-raising walks, Gay Pride Parades or Memorial Day parades?
- Many churches sponsor soup kitchens and food distribution programs but then how many stop and ask why are the people hungry or why they need medical care and places to live?

Taking a stand means taking a risk, trying something new and creative in ministering to the people of God.

Church Divinity School of the Pacific Graduates

In the early 1960s three graduates of the Church Divinity School of the Pacific (CDSP) united to form a joint ministry to continue to bring the gospel to the Mission District in San Francisco. This mostly blue-collar, South-of-Market-Street neighborhood was changing to a more Latin and African-American population. The local Episcopal Church membership was diminishing, and the new neighbors were not easily welcomed into the worship and parish life.

The Diocese under the leadership of The Right Reverend James A. Pike and Archdeacon Darby Betts formed the Episcopal Mission Presbytery. The idea was to band together the four churches south of Market into a Presbytery. Bishop Pike tried to bring Episcopalians and Presbyterians into closer working harmony. The use of Episcopal Presbytery was to symbolize the work south of Market to be ecumenical in nature.

The Episcopal Churches were Church of the Good Samaritan, led by the late Donald Ganoung, CDSP, '61; Holy Innocents, lead by Martin Risard, '57; and St. Barnabas, whose vicar was Lane Barton, '59, out in the Excelsior District.

Church of St. John the Evangelist's rector was the late Edward Berey, General Theological Seminary (GTS) in New York, '56. I was supposed to coordinate the work of the four churches. I was GTS '56.

Our theology was as followers of Jesus we were to minister to the sick, the needy and oppressed. Many people living in urban areas and poor neighborhoods were economically needy and oppressed by the law and racial and ethnic prejudices.

We met regularly for Eucharist and planning, lunch, dinners and family outings. We tried many things to attract and to minister to the wide variety of people in and around the churches.

We held street preaching sessions at the corner of Mission and Twenty-second Streets. John Harms played the trumpet; we had a portable organ, sang hymns and took turns preaching. We held an ecumenical preaching mission in a large Methodist Church with nationally famous Bishop Pike as lead preacher.

The four churches sent children to the Bishop's Ranch in Healdsburg, California. It was the first time many of the children had ever been out of the city. Some saw a cow for the first time. We had religion classes, arts and crafts, sports and, of course, good food. We taught some children to get used to the water and swim in the pool.

College students and seminarians came for summer-service projects in the Presbytery. They had daily Morning Prayer, Holy Communion and Bible study. They branched out into the neighborhood and taught Vacation Bible School. They made calls on newcomers and helped families get in touch with the family services the City provided for food and shelter needs.

One student's father was the Bishop of Idaho. One summer a priest from the Church in Nigeria came and joined the project.

He was Adeneye Ulufumi Olamadosi. He added a black African to the ministry and was popular in the community.

Realizing that many in our neighborhoods were discriminated against, we began to take action. The clergy joined the NAACP, neighborhood groups and community organizations and participated in sit-ins.

In 1964, several of us went to Selma, Alabama, heeding the request from Martin Luther King, Jr. calling on clergy to support the march on Montgomery, Alabama, for freedom of assembly, voting rights and an end to legal discrimination.

In 1965, we joined picketing of the Cadillac Agency on San Francisco's Van Ness Avenue. No salespeople who worked for that agency was African-American or Hispanic. Several of us were arrested and spent an afternoon in jail. Several of us were in a cell with the late Sterling Hayden, movie star and author.

CDSP student, the late Bill Clancy, '64, who had been a lawyer for the U.S. Government, got us out on bail, then raised money from the student body of CDSP to pay the fines we had incurred. The students were very supportive and enthusiastic about the Civil Rights Movement in the '60s.

The clergy in the Presbytery were an interesting and varied lot. The Reverend Lane Barton had fought in the Battle of the Bulge in WW II. He taught Greek at CDSP on a part-time basis while Vicar of St. Barnabas. Lane also marched in Selma. He believed in working with his hands, like Jesus the carpenter, and led the way for the people of the church to physically refurbish and design the church. He went on to be Canterbury Chaplain at Stanford University. He is retired and living in Vancouver, Washington. His late father was the Bishop of Eastern Oregon.

The late Rev. Martin Risard and his wife Alice had owned a travel store in Oakland before he went to CDSP. He helped in buying food and managing the summer service project. He served other churches in the Diocese of California and is retired and living in central California. He led many trips to the Holy Land and Great Britain as an extension to his ministry

The late Rev. Donald Ganoung had served in combat in the Korean War before going to seminary. He focused on the Native Americans in the Mission District and invaded Alcatraz with them in the '60s. He also marched in Selma and was arrested on Van Ness Avenue. He went on to be head of security at Woodstock.

The rector of St. John's really didn't want to be in the Presbytery. He was rector of a parish while the others were mission vicars. So it was hard to keep working together. I had responsibility but no authority. The experiment was vital for three years, but it eventually died out as the clergy moved on to other work. I was appointed executive assistant to Bishop Pike, became Vicar of St. Aidan's and later served as rector of Trinity, San Francisco, for twenty years.

In those days there was not a lot of information about church growth, planting churches and revitalizing churches with rocky futures. We had modeled our ministry after the urban missions in the Lower East Side of Manhattan, Jersey City and East Harlem. Advertising, public relations and gathering names and addresses were not routinely done. We had no idea about targeting an audience; however, the clergy enjoyed some media coverage for our work in civil rights.

Work was also set up in East Oakland under other CDSP graduates with Barry Bloom, CDSP, '62, and John Frykman, a minister of the Lutheran Church. In addition work was established in Hunter's Point in San Francisco, under Bruce Kennedy, '60. He and his wife Daphne actually moved into housing for the poor in that part of the City. He worked primarily as a community organizer with young men and with the Hunter's Point Tenants Union. Bruce's father was Bishop of Hawaii.

St. John's stayed on as a parish and today is an assisted parish with some money coming from the Diocese. Holy Innocents has done well recently with strong ministries under Armand Kreft, CDSP, '86, and Rosalie Harden, CDSP, '99. Bertie Pearson, CDSP, '07, is the part-time priest in charge of St. John's and Holy Innocents.

St. Barnabas became the School for Deacons and was eventually sold to Coleman's Advocates for Children. The Good Samaritan Church and Community Center was torn down and low cost housing was built. The church became the Spanish-speaking mission, El Buen Samaritano, and meets at St. John's.

CDSP must be justly proud of those graduates in the '60s who worked in the poorest and riskiest neighborhoods and moved in with their families to minister to the local people, moving on to the greater Civil Rights Movement. Many recent graduates choose to work in the urban and depressed parts of the Bay Area.

On Christianity

What Does It Mean to Have Christ in You? Many sermons end with the hope and plea that we discover the Christ within us. We expect that Christians have some experience of finding Jesus, being found by God and having a Christ conversion experience. Some religions hold that we cannot be Christian unless we have had an emotional experience of the living Christ. They demand that we accept Jesus as our personal savior.

Some of us come to follow Jesus as a result of our steady education in scripture, theology and the regular attendance at church, where we receive sacraments and participate in the community. That is pretty much my own personal situation. I am a committed follower of Jesus by background, tradition, education and participation in the church. But I cannot say I have been "converted" or had a mystical experience. Many people do testify who have had such a *warming*, to use John Wesley's term. Many have been moved by Billy Graham crusades and accepted Jesus by going down the aisle to have hands laid on them in prayer.

My own commitment to follow Jesus came through my background in the church, education and exposure to prejudice against Jews, Blacks and homosexuals. It just became natural and right to become an outspoken advocate to help end racial, religious and sexual prejudice. It was just the way it was for me and is now too.

I often press preachers to give examples of people who have Christ within them. The easy ones are Martin Luther King, Jr., Mother Teresa, Archbishop Tutu, Dorothy Day and St. Francis. I believe Gandhi, Madame Curie, and Freud, while not specifically Christian, had compassion and Christ-like love to help people.

How about devout Roman Catholics today? Nancy Pelosi and John Boehner have widely divergent views of how to run the government and care for the poor; both are willing to wage war. Are they Christ-like Christians?

First of all no one can judge the value or quality of another person's commitment to Jesus, the Christ although each of us does that in our hearts and minds. We think—he's a good one and she's not. Madonna was a baptized Catholic and now is involved in a sect of Buddhism. Is she Christ-like? Who are we to judge? Some bishops and others are uneasy with Christian clergy and laypeople who profess to be Zen Buddhists. Why not enjoy both Buddhism and Christianity?

Well, I do make some judgments. I have some standards, but I will praise those who live up to my standards and ignore the rest. I judge a person's commitment to Jesus Christ very simply. How does her or his faith work to serve the poor, the sick, the disenfranchised and seek peace in the world? Does the person's spiritual life result in direct service to others?

I know many devout followers of Christ work to earn a living at jobs whose contributions to others' well-being is indirect—insurance, advertising, engineering, real estate, travel, government, retail, wholesale, food, media, finance and a whole host of others. There are doctors and dentists who serve the sick and suffering directly and become wealthy in doing so. Who am I to judge if they have a Christ consciousness. Nurses and medical technicians give direct care to the sick. Teachers, no matter what their religious beliefs may be, give direct care to the development of children's minds and hearts.

Most people in all lines of work have little or no Christ commitment motivating them. Are the devout Christians any better at what they do than non-believers?

We in the church acknowledge that God's Holy Spirit is at work in people and in the world at all times. My atheist, cardiologist friend saves lives and prolonged the lives of many more. The Holy Spirit works through Larry whether he believes it or not.

We who are members of the church, the body of Christ, must mind our own business when it comes to other people's faith and motivation.

I get tired of this era of pop-spirituality we are in, with meditation, labyrinths, retreats, quiet days, prayer groups and daily offices but little action in the church and the world to help the poor, the oppressed and the sick. While Jesus often prayed, he did not call us to develop our spiritual life. He called us to complete the creation by doing our part in bringing in the Kingdom of God.

If we take following Jesus seriously we need to focus on discovering for ourselves what the best way is to serve the poor, the sick and disenfranchised and to seek peace in the world. We proclaim the gospel, and we do the work we are called to do.

The late senator Mark O. Hatfield, Republican from Oregon, was an evangelical Christian and an activist for peace and justice. He put it this way:

Radical allegiance to Jesus Christ transforms one's entire perspective on political reality. Priorities become totally changed; a whole new understanding of what is truly important bursts forth. There is an uncompromising identification with the needs of the poor and oppressed. One is placed in fundamental opposition to structures of injustice and forms of national idolatry. Further there is a commitment to the power of love as the only means to the end.

Hatfield saw that some issues affecting people could only be solved by changing the laws that oppress people. Changes in the law brought about ending legal oppression of Jews and African-Americans. Today a capitalist, medical-care system fails many people in getting health insurance. Now the government must help the poor get proper medical care. Political action to bring about change is part of following Jesus.

> *From the Hebrew Bible we find a simple principle for living well and following Jesus: Do justice, love kindness, and walk humbly with your God.* Micah, 6:8

Many are quiet followers of Jesus without any announcements of their motivation for bringing sick people to church, teaching school, being a social worker and working as a hospital administrator—to mention just a few ways to follow Jesus.

I find it inspiring to see and hear about people who are acting out of the conviction they are imbued with a Christ-consciousness. Preachers using concrete illustrations of Christians following the teaching of Jesus help motivate others to act vigorously in the world.

Christmas Day—Back to Basics

December 25th is the day the Christian churches celebrate the birth of Jesus. son of Mary and Joseph, a Jewish couple who lived in what is now Israel. The Biblical events of Jesus' birth were not written down until at least thirty years after his death References to Jesus as Messiah, Christ as son of God, were added to the story of his birth to show the importance of this child and man in the eyes of the church as it grew from being a Jewish sect to a world religion. The Christmas music and stories so beloved and popular were all written well after the events of Jesus' actual birth. The church was trying to figure out who this man, Jesus, was.

The gospel stories tell the events of this Jewish prophet's life. He preached with knowledge of the Hebrew Scriptures. He healed the sick and called for peace and for help for the poor and oppressed. He expected the end of history to come in his lifetime. He called this the coming of the kingdom of

God when all would be peaceable and perfect. Early Christian leaders began to ascribe to him characteristics such as Messiah and Son of God, which come from the Hebrew Scriptures. He referred to himself in the synoptics as *Son of Man*, in a sense an everyman.

For the next four hundred years after his death the church tried to define who he was with controversies, debates and creeds written to shape basic Christian beliefs. Then the worst thing happened. Christianity became the religion of the Roman Empire. The simple and basic teachings of Jesus, this Jewish man, became subservient to the state. Hierarchies and even worship became elaborate and took on the clothing of royalty, which exists in many churches today.

The message of Jesus, the humble Jewish teacher, healer and prophet became totally corrupted. It was no longer about love, forgiveness and healing. It morphed into power, money and fame. However, great painting, sculpture, learning, architecture, language and music did emerge from the wealth and power of the church. Great acts of love and mercy came with the Franciscans and others, who founded hospitals and orphanages.

The church quickly broke up into denominations, subgroups, cults and national allegiances. The Irish, English, Poles, Germans, and Russians all have their own forms of Christian expression. Many of the changes in the church came about because the church was aligned with some political power. Russian Orthodoxy was at the mercy of the government. The Holy Roman Empire was the church and state as one.

It was not until the founding of the U.S government that separation of church and state became a reality, that the simple message of the man, Jesus, had a chance to breathe more freely. The future of the Christian Church lies in getting back to the basics of what Jesus, the Jewish prophet and teacher, stood for – love, healing, care for the poor and the oppressed and for those seeking peace.

Faith Means Doubt

I am a priest of the Episcopal Church who sits lightly with my church and traditional religion. My father was an Episcopal cleric as is my brother. We were brought up in a conventional home with grace at dinner, Bible stories at bedtime, and Sunday School and church on Sunday. We celebrated Christmas. Easter and Thanksgiving at church. I attended confirmation class and was confirmed when I was eleven. After public schools in Brooklyn, NewYork. I went to Episcopal prep schools as a day student. I often led one or more of the daily chapel services that began our studies. In summer we went to church camps where there were good discussions of God, Jesus and the sacraments. I went along with everything and questioned little.

But it was at camp I discovered some of the clergy and lay leaders had very strong ideas about what one had to believe to be a real member of the church. Was Jesus a man or a God? Was using birth control a sin? Was Jesus truly present in the bread and wine? Should boys and girls refrain from intercourse before marriage? I rather enjoyed the discussions and did not think about them very much. In the Episcopal Church there was and is no place where one is asked to be absolutely specific about one's belief. For instance, it never was demanded of me that I had to believe in a specific view of the nature of God or Jesus. In the creed we says I believe in God, Jesus and Holy Spirit but nowhere do we have to give a precise definition of what that means.

But another dimension of the church's teaching began to creep into my consciousness. The clergy who taught us had no truck with racial discrimination or anti-Semitism. They spoke of the outrage they felt in seeing African-Americans treated as second-class citizens or worse. They spoke of the horrors of the holocaust and the treatment of Jews in our country.

I went to New York University in New York City, for my bachelor's degree in English and Philosophy. There were lectures and fierce discussions of *did God exist* On examinations I had to know the arguments for and against the existence of God. I was asked to give my own views at the conclusion and justify them. As long as my answers reflected that I had read and understood the material, I was graded for that, not on my specific belief.

I really enjoyed that challenge to my conventional faith but never lost my desire to attend church and participate in the Eucharist. I thought more about the validity of traditional belief but not enough to give up those beliefs.

In addition, the liberal Christian clergy, who were chaplains to us college students, helped others and me to a more mature doctrine of God. God was not a grandfather in the sky counting our sins. God was defined not as a being but as being itself. God was seen as the ground of all being. This is the working definition of God that serves me to this day.

In 1953, I matriculated at the General Theological Seminary in Chelsea, part of Manhattan. It was a three-year graduate school to prepare me to become a priest of the Episcopal Church.

The work was demanding, the conversation vigorous and our beliefs challenged by our tutors and professors. We had to know the material and were tested on it. No one ever asked us exactly what we believed. Some students found they could not accept the traditional doctrines and dropped out. I had begun to get the idea that religious teachings were a way of life, a way of looking at life. They were also dynamic and changing.

For instance, sin was simply a description of the way it was in a broken world that had evil in it. A look around me convinced me that was true, the way it was and is. The creation said that the world was good, beautiful and creative. Jesus' emphasis on caring for the sick and needy and standing up to authority was an extremely exciting and important way to be in the world. These ideas lurked in my mind and heart when I came to be in charge of a congregation.

In my first parish I led Sunday services, visited the sick, worked with the youth and thoroughly enjoyed it. In 1962, I moved to San Francisco and worked as an assistant to the Episcopal Bishop. He was a national figure known for bold stands urging the legalization of birth control, an end to discrimination against African-Americans and changes in the worship forms of the church. He told me and some other clergy to start speaking out in public on these and other issues.

I participated in civil rights demonstrations in San Francisco, marched in Selma, Alabama, and helped found the Council on Religion and the Homosexual in 1965. I appeared on local and national radio and television programs on these issues. It was unusual for clergy to be so outspoken on controversial issues. I truly believe that participating in social and political movements that care for the oppressed, the sick and needy is exactly what followers of Jesus are supposed to do. I found myself more interested in being a follower of Jesus than being a church leader.

In addition, Bishop Pike openly challenged the traditional doctrines of the church—virgin birth, bodily resurrection of Jesus and the Trinity. He saw theology as a discussion, not a set of hard and fast positions that had no flexibility. I took on the idea that we think within a tradition. The ancient teachings of the church are just there. We are called to wrestle with them, find meaning in them, enjoy them or cast them aside.

In 1982, I became the rector of Trinity Church in San Francisco. During that twenty-year tenure, I began every sermon with a quotation from the Bible then related that to the teachings of Jesus, of St. Paul, of the great leaders of the Old Testament and to the social, personal and political concerns of daily and national life. I preached and taught the traditional doctrines openly, saying, this is what the church has taught; this is what I believe, and you are free to choose whether you accept it or not.

For instance, I would say on Easter that the church teaches that Jesus rose bodily from the dead. I believe that disciples had some awesome and life-changing experience after Jesus died. They believe he had risen from the dead. Next I would say, you, as intelligent and mature people, get to choose what you believe. I would add that Easter is the time of the year when we see new life emerging all around us in the spring. New life is always available to you to refresh and renew you own life.

Most people liked what I had to say, some people agreed with my views, and I suppose some people did not. I do not remember people leaving because of my views of doctrine.

When I spoke of supporting lesbian and gay rights and same gender marriage, some people did leave. When I indicated I was a pacifist and against war, some people may have left.

I truly believe a lot of clergy believe the way I do but are too fearful to say so for fear that parishioners will leave. Some probably will. But I do believe the truth will make you free. I certainly felt free during my time at Trinity and during my nine years in retirement.

I see the word *God* as a metaphor that stands for being itself, the ground of all being. It is hard to relate to those concepts. I feel fine referring to the words *Father* or *Mother* representing these ideas. The parental terms are also the creative terms. When I pray "Our Father...." I know the word *father* relates to the ground of all being. *Father* or *mother* is more intimate and warm than *being itself.*

I still pray. I do not expect God to answer my prayers in ways that I want. I mostly give thanks for my wife, children, family and friends. When I pray for the sick, poor and oppressed, it is my job to do something about them, not God's.

I have faith. Faith is standing in awe and trust in the presence of the holy. Faith is the awareness of the holy, the sacred, the divine and the sheer otherness of life and the creation. Faith is standing in the presence of not knowing and of the mystery, the horror and delight of human experience. Faith is the opposite of religion, which attempts to confine and define the divine. Faith stands in "readiness...to confess its radical incompleteness and insufficiency—indeed its brokenness."

True faith "begets, besides modesty, the courage to hope, and to work for change."

For me, my faith is nourished by knowing the life of Jesus, attending church, receiving the sacrament of Holy Communion, enjoying the music and liturgy and participating in the religious community. I sit lightly with religion, doctrines, rules and the church. I am grateful that it has been through religion and the church I have learned faith.

Monkey Mind

Monkey minds are bad for you, so goes conventional wisdom of the artists of meditation and spirituality. The monkey-mind races from thought to thought and image to image, stirring up throbbing emotions and passions that disturb the peace and quiet that bring serenity.

Calming the monkey mind will bring stillness and balm to the harried and hurried persons who hurtle through modern or postmodern life. Presumably we will sleep better, think more carefully, become more creative and be better persons. Religious people proclaim that in this calm we may better discern what God calls us to do and be.

The western interest in Buddhism, the religion of much of Asia, has aroused interest in the calming effects of meditation. The Jewish and Christian religions have called on adherents to pray, be silent and hear the *still small voice from within or from God.*

Meditation centers, Gurus, retreats, spiritual directors and fakirs thrive in today's secular and religious world to help people calm the monkey-mind and help us be better people.

Since I was a student in the seminary in the early 1950s, I have been exposed to all kinds of meditative practices. I have failed miserably at them all. I either fall asleep or think of sex. I used to feel bad that I could not calm my monkey mind. My thoughts jump happily from concepts, ideas, schemes, plans, occurrences, notions and ideas. It finally dawned on me that the monkey mind was really a good thing, and I was not going to try to calm it anymore.

I decided to watch my monkey mind when I tried to take a nap, go to sleep, think about writing or planning a trip. The mind gives me ideas and thoughts that jump out at me, and I choose the ones that are interesting, unusual or creative.

Writing with approval about the monkey mind is an example. Thinking about my busy mind made me ask myself what is wrong with the monkey mind? I thought nothing, so I enjoy it.

Putting a theological twist on it, perhaps the Holy Spirit speaks to us through our passionate and ever-changing thoughts. Traditionalists proclaim that the Spirit comes in stillness. Yes, maybe that too.

I have a big problem with my friends and colleagues who spend time calming their monkey minds. I do not see any results from such search for tranquility. I still see a lot of anxious and harried clergy and business people, worried about money, success and advancement. Out of the deep or shallow spirituality that pervades the churches and much of society, I see no passion for justice, peace or concern for the poor. I saw no outcry from the spiritual community when the president openly and cynically allowed more inhuman torture by governmental agencies.

I do hope that many people will get benefit from calming their monkey minds. People who meditate often say they derived great peace from their practice. I am glad this is true for them, but I fear this emphasis on meditation and spirituality keeps people quiet, tranquil and devoid of social consciousness or passion for justice.

On Being a Christian Activist

In my college days at New York University in New York City, I began to make connections between the gospel of Jesus and personal and social behavior. I had seen rank anti-Semitism when I was in high school and in a brief college experience at Colgate University in Hamilton, New York. I heard fellow students talk about "Kikes" and "Hebes." I had already heard about the Nazi death camps and attempts to exterminate the Jews in Europe. Our family had a number of Jewish friends and neighbors. I did not regard Jews as anyone especially different from me. I had also begun to study the literature about the abomination of slavery and knew that was evil. I heard about terrible discrimination toward black people in the South of the United States.

As I finally deeply heard the gospel of Jesus about all-powerful love and forgiveness as the basis for humanity and treatment of human beings, I saw that, if I were to call myself a Christian, I had to connect my beliefs to my personal life, to friends and to the world around me. I saw hate and prejudice, not love and compassion. One summer I was a counselor and waterfront director at a church camp. We had daily church services and Bible study. One counselor, who was studying for the ministry, and I presided at a table with eight children. My friend, Tommy, always took his food first before passing it to the children and to me. He sent out for more food and ate it first. He took the largest dessert. I thought there was something wrong with Tommy's behavior. He saw to his own welfare before he took care of the children—and I. I finally asked him if he thought his behavior was Christian. We chatted about it. He was quiet for a while, but he became less pushy and selfish and shared the food with the others at the table in a more generous and fair way. We both went on to seminary and are friends to this day.

I also *got it* that prejudice against Jews and Blacks was deeply against the ethic of love and compassion as taught by Jesus.

When I was a student at the seminary, I became most interested in the work of the urban priests, who were working in the inner city with the poor and those oppressed in slum housing and those jobless, because they were black and often uneducated. I saw urban social work as a ministry of the church growing out of the gospel imperative.

When I graduated and moved to Bronxville, New York, and served as curate at Christ Church, I was thrust into an upper middle-class neighborhood and parish where the prejudice was constant and genteel. No Jews were allowed in the mile-square boundaries of that town, thirty minutes from central Manhattan on the train. I spoke out against prejudice and was heard then debated politely by the members of the parish. I did yearn to do urban work and be back in the city.

My family and I did move to a parish in the Bronx, Church of the Holy Nativity. Here was a middle-to-lower class parish where the prejudices were much the same as those among the Episcopalians in Bronxville. The church was set in a neighborhood that was sixty percent Roman Catholic and thirty-five percent Jewish. People pretty much stayed with their own kind—with some small cross over. We had Catholic friends and Jewish acquaintances who ran some of the shops.

When John F. Kennedy ran for president in 1960, strong anti-Catholic prejudices emerged. There was some discussion about it among my parishioners. I wore a huge Kennedy-for-President button on my cassock around the church at the coffee hour. It provoked gentle comment, and I found I had taken a stand on a public issue.

A group of peace activists came and spent the night in the church basement. They left the next day for a march on Washington against the growing Vietnam War. I was intrigued by their bravery and fortitude but did not participate.

I had long applauded Bishop James A. Pike for taking a stand for the media, commenting on social and religious issues. He teased the Roman Catholics about movie censorship by attending a condemned movie, *Baby Doll*, with his wife. It was a front-page news story. He supported the right of people to use birth control and was an ardent supporter of civil rights for Blacks and all minorities. The Reveremd Malcolm Boyd was a freedom rider, supporting black rights and using publicity as a white man supporting Blacks. He also wrote books and newspaper articles connecting the gospel of Jesus Christ to what was happening in the world of real human beings.

When I went to work for Bishop James A. Pike in San Francisco, in 1963, he said to other clergy and me that he wanted us to be public in our ministries. He did not want to be the only Episcopalian speaking out on the crucial issues of our time.

He freed me up to write letters to the editor of local and national newspapers. I participated in civil rights demonstrations in San Francisco, and was arrested in a sit-in at a Cadillac agency along with four hundred other protesters. There were pictures in the newspapers and quotes from others and me. I marched in Selma Alabama in 1964, at the call from Martin Luther King Jr. to clergy to support civil rights in the South. Again there was a lot of publicity. There was also a lot of criticism from conservative Episcopalians.

Soon I got involved with the gay-lesbian community in San Francisco. I helped found the Council on Religion and the Homosexual. We criticized the police who invaded a private dance held to support the Council and again got a lot of publicity, support and criticism. I became known in some wag circles as the "fag" priest.

Someone called me the press-release priest. Some said I only did these public stands to get my name in the newspaper and face on television. I suppose there is some truth in that. I did love and enjoy the media attention. I was in demand as a speaker and participant on panels. That enjoyment was a delightful byproduct of relating the work of the church and the gospel imperative of Jesus to the life and people of the City and the world.

For eleven years from, 1970-1981, I worked full time as a marriage and family therapist in private practice in San Francisco. I spoke out for more sex education for adults and for children in schools, further supported rights for gays and lesbians and marched in anti-Vietnam war demonstrations. In my private practice with groups and individuals I focused on teaching good communication skills—full, healthy and free sexual expression and dealing with anger and rage.

From 1981-2001, I was rector of Trinity Church, San Francisco. During those twenty years, I lead the parish to be an open and welcoming church to all people, especially to gays and lesbians. During the HIV-AIDS epidemic we welcomed the sick, ministered to the dying and their families, friends and children and buried the dead. We held seventy-five funerals over the ten worst years of this plague. The parish fed and housed the homeless at various times, especially in winter and rainy months. Project Open Hand used our kitchens for several years before it went out on its own. By the time my years were ending, the members of the parish saw that we were doing what churches are supposed to do as followers of Jesus.

Since my retirement, I have become involved in the peace movement calling for an end to the wars in Iraq and Afghanistan. I stand vigil each Thursday with others in front of the Federal Building in San Francisco.

I think this social and political connecting the gospel of Jesus Christ to the people and times is the elemental work of the church. I see it as my basic vocation. It is my personal and religious response to Jesus and the Biblical imperative. Am I called by God to do this by the devil, by my ego, but my dyspepsia, the desire to assert my masculinity, the desire for publicity, a response to a deep uncertainty about my being? "Frankly, Scarlett, I don't give a damn." This is what I do. I don't have a choice. Sometimes, I think I'll stop going to the vigil for peace and justice. But then I feel like going, and I do. I feel the same way about going to church on Sunday. Sometimes I think I'll just say home and read the paper. The time comes, and I get up and go, even thought the sermons are dull, the liturgy too wordy, and the music thin and uninteresting. I do these things because I do them. Yes, I am a Christian. Yes, I have a bounden duty to do these things. Yes, I'd feel guilty if I didn't.

I am happy to use spiritual or God talk if that helps people. Called by God? Yes. Responding to the message of Jesus. Yes. Is it a spiritual activity? In the silly way spirituality is tossed around these days, I guess I'd say yes. But a *yes* on that level is pretty thin and without much meaning.

I don't have a lot of emotion or feeling or even passion about doing all these things. I get a strong sense of what I want and should do then I do it. So I will let you, my dear reader, decide what to label it. Too much trying to figure out where the impulse for peace and justice comes from is the surest way to paralyze yourself.

Science and the Church

It may come as a surprise to what I call *Spiritual But Not Religious* (SBNR) that many scientists and mathematicians are both spiritual and religious. Two professors at University of California, Berkeley, one in sociology and another in mathematics, are friends of mine who are churchgoers. A professor of criminology at University of San Francisco and two professors of medicine at University of California, San Francisco, are friends and also churchgoers.

If these are people I can pick out of my own immediate acquaintances who are actively involved in mathematics, science and medicine, chances are there are many more still-in-the-closet religionists in that world. This is not to say the halls of academe and medicine are crawling with church and synagogue goers. But I'll bet there are more than one might think. It would make an interesting study to find out what percentage of people in the sciences is religious.

I have never found science and religion to be at odds. Science tries to understand natural phenomena. How did the world begin? Science explores this question by collecting data. Religion is not interested in data; it is concerned with story. The Genesis story is a story told by ancient people about how the world came to be. It was a tale drawn from imagination, awe and wonder. It was not taken from data collected, measured and analyzed. Religion's place is to help people find meaning and depth to their experience of the world. Science's place is to find factual material that shows how the universe and our world evolved over time and space. That exploration in itself is full of awe and wonder, but it is not religion.

Some fundamentalist Christians and Jews insist that the Biblical view of the creation is a matter of fact. The world came into being just the way the Bible says it did in the Genesis story. I think the Genesis story is not science and is not the way the world and universe came into existence. If it is a help and comfort to believe the Genesis myth is the only true way to understand the creation, that is fine with me. I do object to the idea that public schools are forced to teach one particular

44

religious point of view to students of diverse religious and cultural backgrounds.

I also believe science and philosophy have so denigrated fundamentalist religions and made a mockery of their faith that these religionists have fought back with such vehemence. Science, instead of entering into discussion and dialogue with fundamentalist religions, have denigrated their beliefs in the name of being smarter and scientific. Perhaps it is time for serious-minded scientists to enter real discussions with their so-called religious enemies to find a common ground in at least what is taught in public schools and universities.

The most obvious example of the reaction to science by religionists is that the Bible is not allowed to be taught in public schools. Scientists, agnostics and atheists have driven the Bible out of the curricula of public schools and universities. The Bible, taught as literature and a fundamental source of Western culture, can be a way for people to understand where the book came from and how it came into being.

Spirituality

I have a gut-level negative, reaction when I read or hear the word *spiritual*. My mind immediately jumps to a meaning, which cries quiet, inaction, inward looking, selfish, pious, unworldly and irrelevant to the gospel of Jesus.

I have often said and written that the rise of the spirituality movement within the church corresponds with a further moving away from connecting the gospel to the work of the church. The more spirituality, the more justification there is for doing church as administration, keeping the peace and maintaining the institution. Now I must admit that the average parish church and diocese were never and are not bastions of peace, justice, inclusively and concern for change in the society. But now it is even worse.

I have read a couple of books on spirituality, and they all call for deeply spiritual people to minister to the world. I see little response to that level of spirituality. Gandhi, Martin Luther King Jr., Archbishop Tutu and Mother Teresa are deeply spiritual, religious, pious, prayerful people whose work impacted the world. All four said and wrote they were inspired by the gospel of Jesus.

One church administrator I know told me that he thought most graduates of the seminaries these days did not want to go into parish ministry. They want to be spiritual directors. That is a bit of a generalization I will admit. Fewer and fewer parishes offer full time employment to clergy at least in the Episcopal Church. Bishops warn people who think they want to be priests that they probably will not find employment in the church after they are ordained. Yet I think today the local church can be and in fact is the front line of the social and political ministry of the Christian church.

I suppose the spirituality emphasis is another fad in our church life. In the '20s and '30s many clergy flirted with communism and socialism as good ways to serve the hungry and poor, but capitalism won out. I can remember Parish Life Conferences, Group Life Labs, Christian Education, The Seabury Series, Cursillos and now spirituality as ways to save the church. It, too, will pass. One could say that the peace and justice movement in the church is also a fad. Perhaps it is. During a glorious couple of years in the '60s, Christians took action. Many clergy and churches were deeply committed to civil rights, for African-Americans. That commitment thinned out during the Vietnam War and antiwar movement. Except for convention resolutions the present wars in Iraq and Afghanistan are hardly mentioned in church. Full justice for homosexuals still besieges many Christian churches. Deep spirituality must lead to social service and action.

The Church and the City

The Bible starts in a garden and ends in a city, the city of God. The word *city* and the word *civil* have the same root. To be civil is to be human, caring and respecting the will and needs of others. The word *city* today is a dirty word denoting crime, congestion, pollution, danger and poverty. The cities are becoming places of extremes, the very rich and the very poor. The middle classes have fled to the suburbs where the illusion is that it's a better place to raise kids, not noticing the drug use and criminal activity of suburban life.

The cities still are the places of great buildings, grand houses, mansions, opera houses and symphony halls, parks, the best theaters and restaurants, major universities, hospitals, great museums, the financial centers and churches and cathedrals.

Life is on the sidewalks in the city. One can walk to the grocery store, hardware store and coffee shop, even many times to work. No car is needed to engage in the life of the city. Streetcars, buses and subways carry citizens all over the place.

"Eyes on the sidewalk" is an expression coined by Jane Jacobs, late critic of urban life. Neighbors may not know each other well, but they watch out for each other. When my daughter, Jessica, was five years old, she was playing on the sidewalk near a tree in front of our house. I parked my car nearby and walked up to her bent down and began to talk with her. I realized a woman had come up and stood behind us. When she saw I was Jessica's dad, she said, "Oh it's you; that's okay." Her eyes were on the sidewalk; she had not recognized this man talking to this little girl and was just checking up.

More and more city housing is affordable only to the rich and the poor. Flourishing churches and cathedrals in the city minister well to the affluent with numerous clergy; beautiful, well-kept church buildings; good church school curricula and teachers; fine organists; organs and choirs.

Most of the other Episcopal churches have one full-time cleric if they can afford it, a part time organist, volunteer choir—not usually very good—part-time secretary and sexton. Sunday church school and youth groups happen from time to time.

These affluent and marginal churches do a fair job of ministering to the existing congregation, Episcopalians, welcoming newcomers, providing religious education, visiting the sick and shut-ins, baptizing and burying. Sunday services, preaching and programs are usually uninspiring. Parish groups like altar guild, vestry, stewardship committee and worship committee exist and do their work of keeping the parishioners happy and entertained.

Some churches provide social services, such as soup kitchens, shelter programs, and a variety of good and necessary services to the community. A very small minority of the church members carries out the social services ministries.

When I was rector of Trinity, San Francisco, Marilyn Saner ran a shelter program one month each year for ten years. Seventy-five homeless men came to the parish rooms for a dinner and spent the night on cots. Of the three hundred members of the parish, seldom more than half dozen helped serve the breakfast or dinners. That is typical of the response of most church membership to church-sponsored social services.

The great needs of the city are seldom faced and are not met by parish churches. These are justice issues. The difference between social service and social justice is summed up by the quote from Dom Helder Camaro, "When I fed the hungry, I was called a saint. When I asked why are the people hungry, I was called a communist."

Church people are willing to feed the hungry. Church people generally are not interested in the question of why people are hungry or homeless, unemployed or sick or why children are bitten by rats in their homes or why children graduate from high school and can't read or why we have war?

These are justice issues. The civil rights' movement for freedom for African-Americans, homosexuals and women involved many church people. The parish churches urban or suburban seldom, if ever, deal with these justice issues.

My daughter attends an affluent, small-city church and went to service on the Sunday before Labor Day Monday. After the service she said to the preacher, "You missed a good opportunity to refer to the labor movement, unions or work in the sermon or prayers of the people."

Jesus' ministry was to the sick, poor, lame and blind. He gave short shrift to the religious and social leaders of his time.

In weakness there is strength; the poor and the humble shall led the way.

It is by facing and becoming deeply involved in social justice issues that we are truly following Jesus. It is becoming immersed in these issues that we are doing the work of the church and the gospel. I also believe that kind of ministry of intense integrity and real meaning will attract unchurched people to look at the church and find Jesus as the source and energy and basis for a human life that has concrete goals and depth of authenticity.

It was exhilarating and exciting to decide to go public with the slogan, "Gays and Lesbians Welcome in this Church." It went against the will and desire of many members of Trinity, San Francisco, and many Christians in the diocese of California in 1981. It was shocking news to say publicly that our church would be available for funerals of the men who died of AIDS in 1983 when the epidemic was given a name. Many parishes and dioceses finally followed suit. By pushing the church, the church made institutional changes toward justice for homosexual persons.

It was a challenge to the parish and diocese to perform marriages of same gender couples in 1985. We performed such ceremonies, withstanding threats and criticism from the Bishop and many laypersons. The church on the national and international level is working toward full justice for homosexual couples to have the same rights in church and state as heterosexual couples. Candidates for president today have to wrestle with their stands on homosexual rights.

This is social justice as opposed to social service. A few other churches, not many, have taken on important social justice issues. All Saint's Church in Pasadena, California, comes to mind.

Urban churches face many other important social issues. Every major city in the United States has young African-American men killing each other daily, caught up in the drug traffic, poverty and the perceived status of imprisonment. The drug traffic itself is a major issue. Many of us feel legalizing marijuana and other soft drugs would not be deleterious to society, would provide tax moneys for the sale of the drugs and get many people out of the trade. No church to my knowledge has dared to become involved in dealing with these two issues—killing of youths and drugs.

PREACHING

How to Preach a Prophetic Sermon and Get Away With It

In this era of spirituality (what I call *Woo-Woo* Episcopalianism), in the Episcopal Church we seldom hear a prophetic sermon, a message supporting specific issues, social problems or candidates. It is not enough to end a sermon with let's support social justice, act with love or follow Jesus. While all three of these prescriptions are sound and true, they are vague, amorphous and not helpful. These sermons cry out for specificity, a concrete example of justice, an illustration of how to love, a direct action that shows the following of Jesus' words or life.

Preachers are rightly fearful of offending some members of the congregation if they support the right to life or abortion legislation. Urging the rights of homosexuals in church and state will indeed offend some parishioners, which will be reflected in their annual pledges. Opposing or supporting the wars in Iraq and Afghanistan will draw fire from the relatives of military personnel and antiwar protesters.

The result of these fears is lame, vague and safe sermons that do not inspire people to action and do not stir their consciences. Such sermons are dull, thin and lacking in passion or urgency.

In my ministry I have been a strident supporter of African-American and homosexual rights from the 60s to the present. I preach strong sermons based on the New Testament, the law and just plain common sense, justifying full freedom for all people. I used to make people bad and wrong for disagreeing with me. I implied they were unchristian and certainly not followers of Jesus. Deep in my heart I do believe racism and sexism is evil.

However, I found a way to preach my specific calls for justice without condemning those who disagree with me. I began to realize there is ambiguity in all moral situations; there are rational and emotional reasons that make us Christians hold a wide variety of opinions on the same topics. For instance, what is the most just economic system? Capitalism, communism and socialism all have good and bad aspects to them. There are several sides to be taken seriously on abortion. None of them have the whole, unerring truth.

Here is what I do. I amass my arguments for homosexual rights as I see them. God and Jesus love all people in creation. The Biblical proscriptions are subject to a verity of interpretations, just as is the whole of the Bible. Gay and lesbian Christians and non-believers, whom I know, are caring, loving compassionate human beings.

Then I say, "Now I am going to express my own opinion, my personal view as preacher and spiritual leader. What I have to say is not the opinion of God, Jesus, the Holy Spirit, the Episcopal Church, our Bishop, our diocese, this parish or its members. It is my opinion. Please listen to it, evaluate it, consider it then make up your own mind on the subject."

Then I make known my own specific opinion. "I believe homosexuals should have full freedom in church and society, including marriage and ordination, and we should work to change the laws of the state and canons of the church to bring about this full freedom." I usually then re-iterate that "this is my own personal view, and I hope you will develop yours. I am happy to talk with you any time about this or any issue."

I have used this method of preaching on many issues, including candidates I am going to vote for president, governor and mayor. I find people interested in my opinions. They do not feel put down or criticized or judged. People also know that I believe in the rightness of my convictions. They know that I honor their positions while often disagreeing. Many people have given me positive feedback for this kind of preaching.

If preachers have the courage of their convictions and preach them in a loving, non-judgmental way, they will be heard and appreciated. Sermons will be interesting, specific and relevant to the daily life, thoughts and concerns of parishioners and all who listen.

How to Listen to a Sermon: Take Notes

When sermon time comes at worship, do we look forward to it, dread it or hope for insight and understanding of what the scriptures mean? Most of us have not considered how we listen. We can ready ourselves to listen and to understand with our minds and hearts what the preacher is saying.

I have been retired for ten years and have listened to many sermons during that time. In order to focus on what is said from the pulpit, I take notes. In high school and college we deepened our learning by taking notes. I start by recording the time the sermon starts and, later, when it ends.

I listen for the Biblical text. It does not always have to start the sermon. It may come in the middle or at the end. I try to understand the Biblical passages mentioned. Often more than one Biblical reference is confusing to me and makes my mind wander.

At first I jot down everything I hear, summarizing in a few words what the preacher is saying. I look for what the preacher is searching to say, the theme or the main idea. I listen for stories. Jesus was an artist, a storyteller of immense talent. The stories are what most of us remember from a sermon.

I like stories from the preacher's own life—foibles, triumphs, failures and successes. These make me feel connected to the humanity of the preacher. In high school our athletic teams mostly lost our games to other schools. The reality and sad humor of those events made me grow and learn something of the way of real life. People often remarked how much my sport stories meant to them.

A friend wrote, "The other day at the cathedral for ordinations, the preacher told a ubiquitous, Native-American tale. I had already zoned out and was fidgety. It was only when she began to recount personal stories of her relationship with the ordinand that her words interested me, and I became engaged in the sermon. I really didn't know the ordinand, but by her telling personal stories, I felt more a colleague than before."

I write in my notes when I hear the preacher relate the sermon or Biblical passage to something going on in my personal, social or political life. Can we love a terrorist, the members of the political party to which I do not belong or the sixteen-year-old boy who murders his father, mother and two brothers with a pistol?

I note when my mind wanders. I ask myself what happened? When I return to listening closely, the preacher has become vague, lacking the specific and the concrete. She or he is examining a concept, idea or abstraction like the Trinity, Incarnation or the details of the real presence. These important issues are best handled in discussion groups. We listeners can learn from their mention from the pulpit, but it takes real work to pay attention to abstractions for very long.

At the sermon's conclusion I take a moment with this checklist.

- Was there a clear theme that was stated and illustrated?
- Did the stories relate to the theme?
- What did I learn from this sermon?
- How does this text relate to anything in our lives today?
- Did the sermon help move me to be a better follower of Jesus?

- Was I moved to any action by the preacher's words?

I will bet that a preacher who looks up and sees the congregation taking notes will become a better and more careful preacher and taking notes will make the listener a more attentive participant in the preaching enterprise.

How to Listen to a Sermon

A friend, a thoughtful layperson, asked me what criteria I use for evaluating a sermon? Good question. There are few guides for lay people on how to listen to a sermon and what to look for in a preacher's efforts. Here are some items I think are important to keep in mind when listening to a sermon.

- *Length* In the context of Eucharist a sermon should be no longer than fifteen minutes and preferably twelve. A traditional Sunday morning liturgy has four readings from the Bible, Old Testament, Psalms, New Testament and Gospel. (That is far too many for human beings to bear. Most people couldn't pass a quiz on what was in any of them save a really good gospel story, maybe.) Then there is the lengthy Nicene Creed, endless prayers of the people, which in many churches include a boring telephone book list of people in sickness, toil and trouble, most of whom no one has ever heard of. Then there is the long Thanksgiving consecration of the elements, then lines of people taking communion. Fifteen minutes for the sermon is plenty in that context. If the service is Morning or Evening Prayer on a Sunday, a twenty to twenty-five minute sermon might be endurable.
- *Theme* Does the sermon have a central theme or point? Can it be summed up in one sentence? I heard a sermon that dealt with the following themes: The spirit works outside the normal channels, the culture yearns for the spirit, environmentalism, various

uses of salt, ordained through adversity and finding Christ in others. All of the themes were important and helpful for living the Christian life. Any one of them would have made a fine sermon. Dealing with too many themes makes the sermon long, confusing and unfocused.

- *Bible* How does the preacher use the Bible? With four Bible passages to choose from, the preacher has many choices. Sadly many preachers feel they have to mention all four passages, plus a sacrament or two. A good sermon deals with one major theme and one passage from the Bible. It is hard for some preachers to focus on a simple theme that emerges from the scripture. If the preacher bounces around from passage to passage, he or she confuses the congregation. Thrusting the Bible in the face of the people is a way of exerting power over those who respect the Bible but don't know much about it. Lay people may tend to be intimidated by the superior knowledge of preachers who indeed do know more about the Bible than most lay people. The preacher who tosses around lots of Bible references usually has not chosen a clear, simple, major theme to share with the people.
- *Stories* What most people walk away with from a sermon is a good story. Jesus was a storyteller, an artist, who told stories to teach his understanding of the word of God. The Good Samaritan and The Prodigal Son are among the most famous stories remembered by millions of Christians and others. No sermon should end without the recounting of a story *not* in the Bible. The story should be from real life in the world, from the newspapers, about the people in the parish (not the confessional) or about the city and community where people live. To retell a story that has just been read at the gospel is an insult to the intelligence of the listeners. Stories

gleaned from literature, television, movies, sit-coms, theater and songs often reflect the hurts and joys of human life and can inspire Christian people to forgiveness and love. Autobiographical stories help humanize the preacher. A sermon without a story is like a meal without salt.

- *Life Now* A sermon should relate the gospel of Jesus to how we are in the world right now. It should be real and concrete and not airy-fairy, full of ideas and concepts. Love, compassion, forgiveness, healing and community are gospel themes that relate directly to how we treat each other in church, school, work and family. The gospel relates to how our nation acts in the world. How does the gospel relate to race, sex, war, torture, abuse and so many more issues?
- *Call to Action* A good sermon ends in a call to action. The preacher can move the congregation to action in the world based on the social, personal and political issues we all face every day. Write a letter, visit the sick, give money to a cause, teach a child or yell at the president.

I suggest people listen and take notes when listening. It will be much easier to stay awake and will help in understanding what is being said. The structure, or lack of it, of the sermon will be more apparent.

Give the preacher good sermon feedback. Be concrete. Not just, "I liked your sermon," but "I enjoyed your view of the Eucharist, the story of the virgin birth or homosexuality." Or perhaps you disagreed with something specific. Say that.

Most preachers get very little concrete, helpful feedback. Most of us need it regularly. One book I read suggested regular feedback sessions with members of the congregation. Another suggested the preacher sit with people and study the passages from the Bible to be read the following Sunday to help come up with sermon ideas.

Some More on Preaching

I have this urge to write something that will help clergy and lay people improve their preaching. The biggest problems are:

- Too much exegesis of the Bible in the pulpit.
- Too many ideas, concepts and points of view.
- Too vague and amorphous.
- Not concrete and specific.
- Not connected to real life.
- Failing to relate the gospel to social, political and ethical issues.
- Too serious and lacking in lightness and humor.
- Inability to end the sermon. "No terminal capacities."
- Failure to have one basic idea and focus in the sermon.
- Too complex.
- Few preachers use the sound system effectively.

Why write about suggestions to improve preaching? First, good preaching interests me and makes my churchgoing have more meaning and gives me more interest and pleasure. If it please and encourages me, it will do the same for others. Too many sermons are boring; I hate to be bored.

I will go down the list and comment on each of the problems as I see them.

Because four readings from the Bible—Old Testament, Psalm, New Testament and Gospel—are cataclysmically awful enough to sit through, the preacher spending any time explaining the author, date and purpose of the text adds insult to injury. Do as little Bible instruction as possible in the pulpit. Leave that to Bible study, which should be going on all the time in a Christian community.

State the theme from the Bible and get on with it. In the Widow of Nain story, Luke 7:11-17, I chose the theme of hunger—what a widow faces when her son dies and she has no relatives. Jesus raises her son from the dead so she can eat. You can spend time on raising the dead, miracles and the location of Nain in Jesus' ministry or the place of women in Luke. You may be able to find other themes related to the person and social life of your listeners. I chose hunger—personal and worldwide and how we Christians can serve the world. Themes are myriad but choose one not six.

This brings us already to the second point. Choose one idea or concept and stick to it. Do not be tempted to drag in every idea you ever had as you read over the poignant story of Jesus and widow of Nain.

This story lends itself to vague and amorphous ideas— the meaning of death, the miracle of raising one from the dead, Jesus' knowledge of his own power. These themes are interesting and important. They can be related to real life concerns or biblical studies. The preacher must wrestle with one major idea that can be explained and be made relevant in 12-14 minutes.

How can we make our sermons concrete and specific? It means we have to take a stand. In the Nain story, I take the stand that we need to take local and world hunger seriously as loving compassionate Christians. For example, we support the local food bank. Tell a story of a local facility. We need to raise taxes to feed more people at home and abroad. We need to have an excess profits' tax so that the billionaire classes' money can be spread around a bit better. Quote some statistics on how much money some people earn and how much profits oil companies make.

How to Preach Against the Present U.S. Wars

Few sermons are preached opposing the present wars waged by the American Government in Afghanistan and Iraq. Doubtless many clergy oppose these wars. Many Episcopal lay people also oppose them.

Our baptismal covenant calls all of us, clergy and lay people "...to strive for justice and peace among all people." Jesus calls us to be examples of redemptive love and forgiveness. We even call Jesus the Prince of Peace.

We Christians know we are to be peaceful people and makers of peace. We also know that many Episcopalians and other Christians are soldiers, warriors and defenders of the country. Many Episcopalians support the present wars, many in our own parishes. Yet it is imperative that preachers of the gospel of Jesus Christ speak against the present wars, the violence against civilians and the ravaging of homes and cities. Many in the church yearn for the clergy to be moral and spiritual leaders and guide their thinking on ethical issues.

How can we preach against the war and not offend some people, lose members and money and split our congregations? It can be done. It begins with trust. We can tell our people our fears. Be up front; tell them we are afraid our opposition to the present wars will make some people leave, and the parish will lose money."

We need to trust our congregations to be thoughtful, reasonable and loving people despite the variety of opinions they may hold. We can trust them to listen, to be persuaded toward peace or, for whatever reasons, to remain firm in their positions supporting the wars. We must trust ourselves to know what we believe and set it before others fairly and without rancor. We also must not fear our strongest convictions; they may well be what the spirit is calling us to say.

Share with your people that you are opposed to the war. Make sure you indicate that you know others have different opinions and you are open to discussing them. Opposing the war does not have to be a matter of right or wrong. It is a matter that, as a preacher and a person, you are a peacemaker and oppose violence as the way to peace. It is a matter open for discussion.

One preacher said it this way; "I hope that the fact that I am opposed to this war will not mean I cannot serve you as your pastor. I do understand pain, grief and death....Pastoral care will not be dependent on how I feel about the wars."

Even after all that, some parishioners may leave and some money might be gone too. Perhaps, others will admire our courage and join the church and replenish the money. Another benefit of prophetic preaching is that it opens the way for discussions and study groups on peace and other issues of social justice.

I wonder what the country would look like if the clergy and lay leadership of our church spoke openly and honestly in opposition to war and tackled real peacemaking?

Preaching Made Simple

Listen to the Mormon Tabernacle Choir broadcasts, Sunday mornings at 7:30 a.m., KOIT, 96.5 FM, in San Francisco. Especially listen to the regular two-and-a-half minute sermons. The content is pretty schmaltzy, but the form is superb. It is a simple one point and one-illustration talk. It is a fine model for preachers. The speaker chooses one point—love, justice, compassion and so on and tells a short story illustrating the point.

This morning the speaker told the story of a Tony, a Down's syndrome teen who got new clothes to go to the Philippines with his mother. When they got there, they witnessed the aftermath of a hurricane, which left hundreds of people soaked, muddy, torn and injured. After they got to their hotel, Tony went to his room, put on his old clothes and went to the front desk with a plastic bag. He talked haltingly to the clerk and asked that his new clothes be given to the displaced and soaked people who needed them. All were moved by this simple act of love.

Week after week the Mormon speaker finds simple stories to illustrate the point he wishes to make. We Anglican preachers have the luxury of twelve-to-fifteen-minute sermons to elucidate a passage of scripture, find a sentence that summarizes what we want to say, illustrate the point, make a call to action and get it over. The temptation is to get too complex, make too many points and dribble over all four Biblical passage read in the liturgy.

My wife, Ann, is an ethnic Mormon, now Episcopalian, and we both love choral music. Listening to the program over the years, I began to appreciate the skill of the simple preaching.

Robert Warren Cromey

Sermons, Preaching and Such

I have listened to many sermons on Sunday mornings since I retired in February of 2002. Visiting different churches each week gives me a wide picture of what goes on in worship. I have learned new hymns, prayers, liturgical dances and responsive readings. I have looked at art on the walls.

I always eagerly await the sermon. I want to hear how other preachers relate the gospel of Jesus Christ to my personal, social and political life. Sometimes I hear a fine story or illustration. Other times I get an insight into human nature and a hope for spiritual development. Mostly I get little that relates to my daily life. I find that I listen best when I take notes on the sermon during the preaching time. I also time the sermon. Here are some observations I have made.

If there are four passages from the Bible—Old Testament, Psalm, New Testament and Gospel, many preachers have the need to salute all four in the sermon. Now I have three years of Biblical training in seminary and have read the daily offices irregularly for forty-six years. If you gave me a pop quiz at the end of the service, I could not tell you what all four or even two were about. This is Biblical overload.

When the preacher tries to tie them all together I get further confused. I am certain that the untrained lay person also swoons with too much information to assimilate. It is bad enough to have to listen to four Bible readings and worse to have to listen to them explicated.

There seems to be the desire of many preachers to do Biblical exegesis in the pulpit rather than in the study. When half the sermon is spent rereading or retelling the Gospel story then explaining its social, political, archeological, Greek, Hebrew, theological and historical context, preachers have not done their homework. Taking one simple idea from the scripture and relating it to life today with a couple of good illustrations and stories is plenty. This will also keep the sermon within the twelve-to-fifteen-minute time slot that fits today's liturgies.

Now I know we were all taught that sermons should have three points. If we can get our parishioners to listen one point well illustrated, we are doing quite well. An old friend used to complain when people told him he preached too long. He said that *Sermonettes* make *Christianettes*.

Another thing I notice is that too many sermons remain too theoretical and lack concrete illustrations or stories. If I find my mind wandering during the sermon, it is always because theory and philosophy are being trumpeted. Lengthy discourses on the incarnation or the doctrine of the Trinity bore quickly. Illustrations of how the enfleshment of God applies to my life are exciting. The incarnation means our physical bodies are important. That discussion holds my interest.

When I hear that the Trinity means that the nature of God unfolds in my life in my head, heart and body, I pay attention. How these great doctrines of the church affect the personal life of the preacher make the sermon exciting.

I also note that few preachers are willing to take a stand on social and political issues. Preachers may mention Iraq, marijuana, abortion or homosexuality but seldom state their own personal opinions. They may fear offending members of the congregation who disagree strongly with the preacher's position.

The preacher can simply say, "My personal opinion is that a woman should have free choice whether or not to have an abortion. This is not the opinion of God, Jesus or the Episcopal Church. It is my personal opinion. I also believe that many of you in the pews may have a different opinion, and perhaps we can talk about it after the service." One can state an opinion strongly and not make other people bad and wrong. The preacher can give others room for their own positions. I think it is important for preachers to make their own positions clear. That is a quality of leadership. It helps people define their own opinions.

When I preach on a controversial issue, I usually say that all of us with widely differing opinions come to the holy table to eat and drink in the mystical presence of Christ, the true source of our unity. Our differences can be honored as we commune with God and each other.

Incorporating these ideas into sermons will help hold my interest and inspire me. I suspect that such an approach to preaching will sustain and excite listeners to a greater understanding of what preaching is about and more important, nourish their spiritual, personal and political lives.

Take a Stand

A cleric asked an African-American veteran of the civil rights struggle if he saw the church as a light in the movement for freedom. He replied "Yes, a tail light."

Christian clergy and lay people often fail to take a stand, a clear position on the major issues of our time. Church groups are still falling behind in the struggle for homosexual rights and same-gender marriage in our country.

Few will take a stand on the policies of Israel toward the Palestinians. Prostitution, drugs, pornography and abortion are subjects seldom addressed by churches and leaders. I believe the church will come alive if the leadership provides thinking leadership and discussion of important issues.

Anti-Semitism. Discrimination against Jews is morally intolerable and personally abhorrent to me. Jewish stereotypes of all types are made absurd by the enormous differences in personality, value systems and appearance among Jews. Slurs against Jews should be challenged by all thoughtful people, especially those who call themselves Christians.

Israel. Israel exists and I support that. I do sometimes wonder about the wisdom of setting up the state in the first place.

Israel vs. Palestine. I am vigorously opposed to the treatment of the Palestinian people by the Israeli government and the majority of the Israeli voters who back that government. I, with a minority of Israeli citizens, regard the policies as brutal, violent and lacking in willingness to seriously negotiate with the Palestinians. I believe there should be a separate Palestinian state.

Some say the anti-Israeli policy toward the Palestinians is the new anti-Semitism. I am totally and completely against the American policies in Afghanistan and Iraq and in most of the rest of the world. Yet I am proud to be an American. I am not anti-American.

I resent that the U.S. government gives billions of dollars a year to Israel. This issue is never debated or challenged by our senators, representatives or the president. They are afraid of offending Jewish voters who comprise the wealthiest minority-voting block in the country on the issue of Israel. The idea of the wealthy Jewish voting block comes from a Jewish friend, a political adviser.

Holocaust. The attempted extermination of Jews and others in death camps in the 1940s is a horror never to be forgotten. Continuing education of young people about the holocaust is necessary. I do believe the holocaust industry has so overstressed the horrible story that it has cheapened it and made the story less horrible by constant repetition of that history.

Preaching Fun

Notes for Fun and Reflection: Some Practical Considerations
- Put in your hearing aid.
- Take your Ipod out of your ears and turn off the ball game.
- Pretend you are interested.
- Act as if you care.
- Don't bang your head on the pew in front if you nod off.
- Sit on the bulletin unless you are using it to take notes.
- Go to the bathroom before the sermon starts.
- Take the gum out of your mouth.
- Put your purse on the floor.
- Do not comb your hair during the sermon, no flossing either.
- Take your eyes off the stained-glass windows; they have been there for one hundred and eighty-five years.
- Oh yes, I almost forgot. Listen to the words.

Dr. King gave the best advice I have ever heard about preaching. He said: Make them laugh, make them cry then tell them what you want them to do.

When I was a new, young priest I was gratified to see a young girl in the congregation carefully taking notes during my sermon. When I complimented her after the service about listening so carefully, she told me she was keeping track of whether I used every letter of the alphabet in my sermon.

From *Barchester Towers*, by Anthony Trollope

"No one but a preaching clergyman has, in these realms, the power of compelling an audience to sit silent and be tormented. No one but a preaching clergyman can revel in platitudes, truisms and untruisms yet receive, as his undisputed privilege, the same respectful demeanor as though words of impassioned eloquence or persuasive logic, fell from his lips."

From Bryan:

If this were part of a listening series, then it could be worth writing this way. Otherwise, I would change the title. Keep it, *How to Listen to a Sermon*. It is much more provocative and allows for a wider topic.

You could still have taking notes be part of your discussion, but not the title. Take notes would be the second point.

The first point, is preparing for a listening. Before going to church. What is on our minds? What is going on in the world, the church calendar and the Bible? Is it Lent? What is the priest thinking about? Do we have a guest? How does a priest prepare? There is much to consider before getting to the note taking. I love note taking, but that is the middle of listening.

The middle of the sermon is the sermon itself. Sometimes furiously taking notes, other times drifting on a good point or a boring sermon. How would I deliver the sermon, or how would Cromey do it? How does this point apply to myself? What will I have for dinner? All these questions.

The end is afterward. A good sermon is looking at the notes or listening to a tape then re-listening and applying to life. To me, the sermon is the best part of church.

From Andy:

Thank you for this lesson in sermons, and in asking for my comments. I had a dream the other night that God told me you had died, that you had been shot chasing a person who tried to steal something from you. (Ann, in the dream, said you chased him because you had been raised in the Bronx.) The deep grief I felt in the dream, I believe, was not just an indication of how I would feel if you really did die (I know, I know, someday, but not today) but the grief of losing Trinity as a whole. I realize that, when you and Rob were there, and later David Forbes, a spiritual intelligence was the norm, both coming from the altar, pulpit, and several in the congregation. Your essay instructions here remind me of that spiritual intelligence you embody. Now, I know no one at Trinity but you would have taken notes on a sermon, but there were several folks there with whom I could talk to afterward about some topic or point you, Rob or David had made. I have yet to find a community that takes the depth of a sermon or the liturgy as a whole to heart and comes away contemplating what has just happened.

I might point out that, personally, I often drifted off because of some point that you or others made that triggered a train of thought—then, of course, I often missed some other point, but at least I was sparked, which rarely happens in sermons and liturgies these days, at least in the places I've gone.

I think the only time a Biblical text should be discussed in a sermon is when it speaks to our every day lived lives—such as preaching with the Bible in one hand and the newspaper in the other. Vettle-Becker's shortcomings, one of oh so many, was preachy preaching—get right with Jesus through the scripture of the day. A guy named Donald Nichol wrote that we cannot understand a gospel story if we haven't experienced it, and I believe it.

I find that often I can tell what the template is for a sermon. First the statement is re-stating the scripture at hand or telling what it means, then the preacher's story about him or herself, then back to the scripture. Preaching is performance, just like teaching. I would suggest required drama courses for all candidates for the clergy.

Jesus, this is typical of Cromeyness—so many thoughts triggered by your words. I hope I haven't blathered on too long, but, if I have, I know that you, like Jesus, will forgive. I like what you have here—it could be applied to teaching as well as preaching. Today I mentioned your statement about being on a team that usually lost to the other schools, and I could see that the kids here on the teams that lose a lot perk up. You should be a teacher. Thanks for this opportunity to think, and write.

From a friend:

> I like stories from the preacher's own life—foibles, triumphs, failures and successes

> Often clergy are shy of telling stories about themselves, especially stories that may put them in a bad light. However, the listener knows that no one is perfect and may feel closer to the preacher who takes the risk of being transparent and vulnerable.

> Before women could be ordained in the Episcopal Church, I hired a United Church of Christ woman minister to lead our Christian education program in

the Santa Monica parish. The Rev. Dorothy Hill was an authority on early childhood education, a gifted teacher and a published author.

A few years later Dorothy and her husband moved to Omaha where he had been given a job as a university librarian. On her last Sunday with us, Dorothy preached. She told the agonizing stories of the treatment she had received as a pioneer, ordained, woman minister and of some of the heartaches in her personal life through the years. The congregation was in tears. I couldn't help but think of how much more support she would have had during her time with us and the added stature she would have enjoyed if that had been her first sermon with us, instead of her last.

Interest soars when the preacher begins a story from her or his life. Nearly everyone agrees with you when you say: I like stories from the preacher's own life—foibles, triumphs, failures and successes.

Politics vs. Values

I chatted with Sonia about her religious background, which turned out to be Episcopal membership but no longer active. She went to a church for a number of years where the rector gave brilliant, intellectually stimulating sermons, and she just loved the experience. When he left, she shopped around for other churches but found few preachers used much of their brains in their preaching. She found them dull, boring and uninteresting.

My wife, Ann, said, "Well you should have come to hear Robert preach; he really is good." Sonia replied, "Well I don't come to church to hear about politics."

I knew the preacher that Sonia likes. His clever, well-crafted sermons reflected Jungian psychology and Christian theology. I never heard him preach, but I read a few of his sermons and thought they were quite good. As a star preacher in the '60s and '70s, he was revered, and his church was very popular. During his tenure in the San Francisco parish, he never referred to the civil rights movement, war, capital punishment, the lesbian-gay-rights movement or any of the major issues of our time. I dare say he helped many people feel better about themselves in a chaotic world, and that was a good thing.

The relationship between religion and politics has been a sore issue in the church since its Biblical beginnings. Christianity became the state religion of the Roman Empire at the time of Constantine. Popes crowned kings. As time went on the relationship between church and state changed and developed right down to the idea of separation of church and state in the U.S. Constitution. The debate continues to this very day as we see right-wing Christians exerting a powerful influence on American politics.

There are always voices in parish churches saying, they come to church for comfort, solace and escape from the demands of work and family. They don't want to hear about politics." When I was a curate in a parish in Westchester County in New York, the community prided itself in keeping out Jews and African Americans. No realtor would sell to a member of a minority group.

In the early 1960s, the growing civil rights movement emerged in part from the African-American churches and labor unions. One Episcopal Bishop in the South told his clergy that they had no business getting involved in the movement for civil rights for all. One California rector said if he had to chose between money and the civil rights fight, he would choose money. He was a good fundraiser and knew how to please his donors. Recently, a prominent San Francisco parish told an Episcopal lesbian-gay group not to send any more offers to conduct a class for his church on homosexual rights.

I wish I had thought to tell Sonia that I see a big difference between politics and values. The Gospel of Jesus Christ is embedded with certain core values—love, forgiveness, community, compassion, reconciliation and healing.

Politics is the art of passing legislation and laws by elected representatives.

The repression of the rights of African-Americans, homosexuals, women and any people flies in the face of Gospel values. It is from love and compassion that Christians urge the passage of laws ending discrimination against any group. It is out of love and forgiveness that the Episcopal Church in convention opposes capital punishment.

Our right-wing Christian bothers and sisters have a sense of love and reject killing unborn babies; they oppose abortion. Other Christians out of concern for the welfare and health of the woman approve of some level of abortion. Christians will disagree on how to express their values politically. But our Christian values are what we stand for; they are the basis for our moral judgments.

Churches and preachers that stand for the spiritual values of comfort, peace of mind and happiness fall short of the challenge of the Gospel to bring love, compassion and community to the people of the world. The churches of the 1960s were called the *comfortable pew*. And Martin Luther King, Jr., said 11:00 a.m. on Sunday morning is the most segregated hour of the week. Sadly this is still so.

We need to reawaken the idea of the church militant who goes forth into the world and works for peace and reconciliation between people, using the political system as needed to bring all in love and charity with their neighbors.

Remember that Thou Keep Holy the Sabbath Day[3]

Thirty-four years ago was the last time I preached from the pulpit at Grace Cathedral. It was a sermon saying that the church needed to minister to our homosexual brothers and sisters. That, since, has been the cornerstone of my ministry. But I am not going to talk about that today.

---

3 A sermon by Robert Warren Cromey; Rector, Trinity Episcopal Church; San Francisco, California; preached at General Confirmation; Grace Cathedral; April 18, 1998.

Congratulations to all who are about to be confirmed, received and reaffirmed as full members of the church. I am going to give you some advice about being a member of the church. I know from experience that no one ever listens to advice, so I might as well give it anyway. Worship God in the church every Sunday. It is not a rule. No one can enforce it. We have no Sabbath police. Only you can decide to do it. It is a standard that you shoot for.

Frankly, God does not give a hoot if you go to church or stay home. (Annie Dillard said something like that.) Going to church works on you, not on God. You go to church for your own good. Going to church makes you a better person and teaches you how to live in this life. It gives you the most important values you will ever learn—to love, to forgive, to have compassion and to live in community.

Worship God each Sunday in the church. Now don't get legalistic on me. In forty-one years as a priest I have heard all the excuses. Sure if you are out of town, you could find a church in which to worship. If you are sick in bed you could pray, read the Bible or even call the church and ask for a lay Eucharistic minister to bring you the sacrament. At Trinity we have more lay Eucharistic ministers than we do sick people.

When I was a kid in Brooklyn, New York, the neighborhood was largely Roman Catholic. The Roman Catholics of my childhood went to church every Sunday. If they were away from home, they found a church and went to it. They went to heroic efforts to attend Mass.

My Mormon relatives have Bible readings and prayers on hiking and backpacking trails. If you choose, you can find a way to be in church every Sunday. Remember church works on you, not on God.

If you go to church every Sunday, you will hear and feel how to behave in the world. As a worshiper and a follower of Jesus Christ, you'll sense the injustice of using the words, *homo, fag, nigger,* or *kike.* You and I will work for justice and peace among all people. We will become aware of the dignity of all humans.

You'll feel for the boy or girl who is shunned, left out of the in-crowd—the nerd, the geek and the odd ball. The boys who took guns and killed four kids and a teacher in Jonesboro, Arkansas, were outcasts, the odd ones in their school. What might have happened if some of the other kids had really reached out to them and gave them a hand? Who knows?

If you go to church every Sunday, your life will change, deepen and be more powerful. You will begin to hear God's will entering your consciousness from the Bible and the Holy Communion.

You won't always like going to church every Sunday. You'll be bored sometimes. I get bored going to church. I even get bored with my own sermons while I'm preaching them. But if you dedicate yourself to going to church every Sunday, you will find out what is truly valuable in your life and in life in general. Here are some more valuable things you will learn.

Money, wealth and power are good and necessary. By going to church every Sunday you will see how God wants us to use that money, wealth and power. You will discover that you cannot worship money, no matter what the television, magazines and business world tell you. Your life won't work if you worship money.

I met a woman on a plane who said, I have all the money, clothes, CDs, cars and furs I need yet I feel empty, and my life has no meaning. She said that maybe finding God and church would give her some sense of meaning. I encouraged her to try.

You will see money as a gift from God, and it can be used for God's work in the world—feeding the hungry and caring for the poor and the sick as Jesus did.

Going to church every Sunday will humanize you. You can't choose the folks you go to church with. It is not a private club or fraternity that discriminates against people by race, gender or sexual orientation. In church you mix with whatever people turn up and learn to love and respect those other odd folks who turn up Sunday by Sunday.

You youngsters—if you want to drive your parents crazy, insist you all go to church every Sunday, somewhere, no matter what. Going to church every Sunday will be a way for teenagers to rebel against the parents who are drop-in churchgoers.

Kids in communist Russia went to church on Sundays, because their Communist parents didn't. It was not permitted under the law. Going to church was a way to rebel.

A member of Trinity feared telling her Swedish parents she went to church, because she was afraid they'd think she was nuts and disinherit her. She felt like a rebel. Going to church will open you to God. Learn to hear God's will for you. You will learn to love—sexually, intimately and caringly—the girl or boy, the man or woman of your choice. How? By knowing that the sensual feelings you have are gifts from God to be expressed and shared. Your pastor, teachers and parents can help you to live intimately. You might even get some decent sex education.

Going to church every Sunday you will learn to love your enemies—Saddam Hussein, the Republicans, the Democrats, those people you want to write off. Even I—a knee-jerk, bleeding-heart, liberal—love my Republican relatives and my Salt Lake City conservative in-laws. It isn't easy, but I learned in church to love my enemies.

When you go to church every Sunday, you will learn that you do not have to be perfect. You don't have to strive for excellence. In a broken and sinful world, you won't be perfect, and you won't be excellent. Sometimes you will be great and wonderful. Other times you will fail and feel broken and a mess. And that is okay. You pick yourself up and move ahead.

If you go to church every Sunday you will learn to love yourself. You will learn that you are worthy, worthwhile, lovable, and forgivable. You will learn to love yourself as you learn to love your family, friends and neighbors.

Our Gospel is that God so loved us that he gave his son for us. When we know we are loved by God, we can love our neighbors, love ourselves and love God.

So remember to keep holy the Sabbath Day and worship God every Sunday in the church.

I Want to Follow Jesus

That is the line from a corny hymn in the Hymnal 490 that I just love. It makes me cry every time it is sung. It reminds me of a priest friend who loved the hymn; we sang it at his funeral. He felt he was a failure as a priest; he just wanted to follow Jesus. He was a poor administrator, fundraiser and group leader. He was a superb pastor, friend and caregiver. He celebrated Eucharist with grace and sincerity and was a fumbling preacher with a deep heart. He started each sermon by saying, "Lord help me make sense about what I am about to say." He paid me the highest compliment by saying that being a priest volunteer at Trinity, San Francisco, when I was rector, was the best job he ever had in the church. He could be himself, be a priest and follow Jesus.

When the Holy Spirit and I decided I was to become a priest, my father was my first role model. A good preacher with a nifty sense of humor, a caregiver feeding homeless men in the parish house of St. Michael's Church in Brooklyn, New York, in the depression years. He counseled young men in the military during the war years, was a prison and hospital chaplain, took funerals from funeral homes to make some extra money and was good with bereaved families. In parishes he was a poor administrator, impatient with the trivia of vestry and most church group meetings, careless with money and wildly disorganized in church and personal affairs. I believe he just wanted to follow Jesus.

The clergy I knew when I was at church camp and later in college and seminary were at the forefront of civil rights for African-Americans. Father Welty, a white Southerner, said he would be happy if his white blond daughter married a black man if they were aware of the social consequences that would have to face. This was in 1950, in an Episcopal Church camp. At NYU the chaplains and visiting clergy speaking to our Canterbury Club not only advocated full freedom for Black Americans but also showed deep concern for the poor, the homeless, the alcoholics and the plight of the inner cities. Some clergy even then were working quietly to counsel and give support to homosexuals. This is what it meant to follow Jesus.

Dean James Pike, of the Cathedral of St. John the Divine in New York City, spoke out in favor of birth control, abortion rights, against censorship by the government and Roman Catholic Church and in favor of the state of Israel. Many Bishops, seminary professors and clergy supported these views but often criticized Pike, because he was in the news all the time. In these formative years speaking out for human rights in public was what it meant to be a follower of Jesus.

In seminary we studied the Bible thoroughly and learned it was a library of different kinds of books. Myth, history, laws, biography, propaganda, worship and mysticism were all found in the book. Yes, it had laws for the ancient Israelites, but it had the thrust of redemption, reconciliation and love. Yes, there was a lot of condemnation of specific people at a specific time in history. It was and is treasure trove of religion not law. In fact it says that we are to be free from the law if we are to be truly human and humane.

When I was ordained deacon and priest I wanted to follow Jesus according to the rules and regulations of the church, which asked me to care for the rich and poor, administer the sacraments and, as a deacon, "to interpret to the church the needs hopes and concerns of the world."

In my first cure as curate at Christ Church, Bronxville, NewYork, I was in charge of the Church School, Youth Group, hospital and parish calling and participating in the liturgy. I led a Bible study group for the church schoolteachers and did a good job of helping them below a literal interpretation of the book. Buy word and example I did the work and fun of following Jesus. We invited a speaker to talk to the young people about alcoholism and AA. Many parents kept their teenagers at home not wanting them associating with alcoholics. Members of the parish also supported the real estate businesses in town by keeping out Jews and Negroes from this all-white community.

In my next job as rector of the Church of the Holy Nativity in the Bronx, I felt I was following Jesus pretty well by preaching, teaching and example then I had a capital-fund campaign to raise money to fix the lead in the stained glass windows. Was that following Jesus? Fundraising took a lot of time and energy from following Jesus. There was opposition to allowing peace marchers to spend the night in the church rooms while en route to a demonstration in Washington, DC. Somehow some members didn't see marching for peace as following Jesus.

My family and I moved to San Francisco when I went to work in the Bishop's office. I was to coordinate the work of clergy and laity in four city churches. I was a community organizer with no training or skills, and the experiment failed. I did get involved in the homosexual rights movement. After founding the Council on Religion and the Homosexual in 1964, others and I were widely criticized for getting involved with gays and lesbians. How could we Episcopalians get involved with people like that? I guess that's what happens when one becomes a follower of Jesus.

I assisted the Bishop in answering his fan mail and working for the diocese as a bureaucrat. I was not following Jesus by my lights.

I became Vicar of St. Aidan's Church in San Francisco, and led the parish in involvement in the civil rights movement, with farm-worker's rights and against the war in Vietnam. We were following Jesus.

I was not following Jesus in my personal life. Our family suffered through divorce, and I became a bachelor for eleven years. I became a therapist and followed Jesus incognito by counseling families and individuals helping them deal with anger, sex, relationships and family life. I was helping well people to get better and to find a loving humanity beneath surface anxieties and tensions.

In 1981, I became rector of Trinity Church, San Francisco. I led the parish in following Jesus by being open to gays and lesbians and by ministering to many, many men who died of AIDS. The parish rallied behind partners, parents, wives, children and grandparents of young men suddenly facing death.

In having an open ministry with homosexuals, we received much criticism from church people and those outside the church about "those" people. Following Jesus means caring for the outcasts of society.

When gays and lesbians wanted to marry in the church, we found that church law was against such unions. Not being one to follow evil laws, I allowed and participated in their weddings and have done so my entire ministry. I actually performed my first church wedding for two lesbians in 1968, at

St. Aidan's, San Francisco. I want to follow Jesus. Many in our church around the world do not see marrying and ordaining homosexuals as following Jesus.

At Trinity we had fifteen AA groups meet each week in the parish rooms, housed and fed seventy-five homeless men during winter months and sponsored a Meals on Wheels Program feeding seniors in the church rooms.

I have become a critic of Israel's treatment of Palestinians and write letters to the editor of local newspapers, pushing that view. Against the war in Iraq, I stand vigil each Thursday in front of the Federal Building in San Francisco protesting the killing in that country.

Some bishops get rid of clergy who have been divorced; one bishop gets rid of clergy who have been divorced three times. Three strikes and you're out. The law becomes more important than the person. Divorce three times is now the unforgivable sin. The image of the church is more important than the face of the crucified Christ.

Following Jesus for me means taking care of the poor and needy, providing homes for the homeless, fighting against capital punishment and supporting the rights of women and those under the heel of the powerful. It often means flying in the face of the rules of church and society; it means being unpopular and notorious. Well, I guess, that what I mean when I say I want to follow Jesus.

Because I was the preacher last Sunday, here are some ideas to help us evaluate sermons we hear when we attend church. Preachers seldom get much concrete feedback from hearers. Perhaps people think it unnecessary or impolite. Some may feel they lack any criteria to judge a sermon. Here are some items to help the hearers evaluate the preacher's offerings.

- Did the preacher have a point to the sermon? Did you get it and understand it? What was it?
- Did the Biblical material used help make the point or obscure it?
- Did you a have a *take away* from the sermon? Were you moved to an action?

- Did the sermon touch you emotionally?
- Did the sermon stimulate your thinking?
- Jesus was a master storyteller. Did you hear a story? Was it connected to the point the preacher was making?
- Did the sermon relate the gospel of Jesus or the teaching of the Bible to your personal, social, political, psychological or religious life?
- What did you not like about the sermon? Example?
- What did you particularly like about the sermon? Example?

If there is no time to give thoughtful feedback after the service, perhaps an email or regular-mail letter would help focus your thoughts. Preachers can learn from what hearers think and feel about sermons. Sermons can best improve when preachers know how their words are heard and understood.

Inspiration or Cogitation in Sermons

Anglican sermons are boring. They are long on cogitation and short on inspiration. The sermons lack passion and preachers lack conviction. Now those are sharp criticisms and fail to note some exceptions. In the ten years I have been retired I have heard a lot of sermons while sitting in the pew. I am shocked at how few were inspirational and sadly, how few had any serious intellectual content either. I seldom have heard a serious doctrine or theory to cogitate on, nor heard a call to action. Because my wife was raised Mormon, we have attended family events in Salt Lake City, Utah, over the years. The sermons and talks I heard in the wards and on the radio were always inspiring, heartfelt, personal and moving. I'll admit few were intellectually stimulating.

Here is an example of a talk in a Mormon church one morning. A husband and wife were the assigned speakers, and they were given a specific idea to speak on. This Sunday it was how "God helped me make a decision." The young woman talked about how she and her husband decided to have a baby while he was still in dental school. God helped them make that decision, she said. She told two other short moving personal stories about how she made decisions with God's help. The young man told two stories and, when he got to the third, he had tears in his eyes. He did not think California Proposition Eight banning same-sex marriage was a good thing. His Bishop, the equivalent of the rector or vicar, asked him to head a church committee supporting the ban. The young, man struggled with his decision but said that God helped him do what his Bishop said to do. That talk or sermon was powerful and moving to us even though we totally disagreed with the anti-same-sex marriage sentiments expressed.

Two things made the talks powerful and inspiring. There was a specific point. God helps us make decisions. There were real human stories. We were moved by the power of the stories—painful, sad and joyful.

Jesus was an artist, a splendid storyteller. He did not preach theology. He told the story of getting the cow out of the ditch on the Sabbath. The Good Samaritan and the Prodigal Son are among the most powerful stories in all of western civilization. Even the Sermon on the Mount was not a sermon but Matthew's collection of various pithy teachings of Jesus.

In Salt Lake City I went to the Episcopal Cathedral. The preacher spoke of the Biblical material, the liturgical reference, but never gave a story or a personal reference. The call to action was that we should keep the Sabbath day as a day of rest. No suggestions on how to do it in a new or creative way. No story on how she keeps her Sabbath. In short no inspiration, no cogitation—not even information on how to keep the day of rest and worship in a busy world.

In the Saturday newspapers in Salt Lake City there are four pages of church news. Mormon news dominates, as it is the most populous church in that city. The news and announcements were inspirations, full of stories and events exciting the members to worship and do good works.

However, in the announcements, ads or talks there were no announced Bible Study groups and discussion groups, and there plainly was no room for doubt or social and political reflections on Christian theology or ethics. We do have that in our Episcopal Church, and I rejoice in that. But the connection with the cogitation is seldom reflected in the sermons that come from the pulpit.

We can learn from the Mormons about our preaching. Select a text from the Bible then select a specific theme or point. Illustrate the point with stories from literature, movies, television programs, newspapers or your own personal experiences. Connect the theme to a social or political event known to the congregation.

- *Text.* Whoever does not carry the cross and follow me, cannot be my disciple."
- *Theme.* The cost of being a follower of Jesus.
- *Stories.* Find and tell a story about not being popular. Find another one about people being ridiculed for their faith. Find and tell story about how a person is free by being a follower of Jesus.
- *Call to Action.* Write a letter to a judge who is deciding a capital punishment decree. Join a demonstration that is against war. In your men's or women's group or book club talk about the cost of being a Christian and follower of Jesus.

That should pep up the sermon and members of the congregation.

The Mormons are long on inspiration, and they are growing and attracting people.

Anglican sermons can be very thoughtful, imaginative, personal, specific, full of stories and applications to the real lives of the people, and thus very inspirational.

A Radical Approach to Improving Sermons

Sermons in the Episcopal Church these days have little or no reference to social, personal or political issues either. Perhaps it is true in other denomination too. I have some ideas for clergy to improve preaching.

First, do not refer to the Bible. Discussion and explanation of the scriptures belong in study groups not in the pulpit. Most people sitting in the pews have little idea of what is in the Bible and most could care less. The references usually are confusing and produce guilt, because people think they should know the Bible but don't.

Second, listen to the Mormon Tabernacle Choir that usually comes on the radio on Sundays. Here is the Bay Area of San Francisco it is on at 7:30 a.m. at 96.5 FM. Go to http://www.mormontabernaclechoir.com/ to listen to past programs on the tab *Music and the Spoken Word*. Listen to the spoken word. Neither the *Bible* nor the *Book of Mormon* is mentioned. The speaker gives an inspirational, often squeaky, sentimental message. He usually tells a simple story that is easily remembered. It is almost always the gospel incognito. It is there, but it is not discussed or analyzed. Its essential meaning is the *take away* from the sermon, what people remember and may use in their lives.

Third, unlike the Mormon speaker, connect the Biblical message to a social, political or personal issue that relates to the parishioners. The Academy Awards are on people's minds. A sermon about rewards and appreciations would have been appropriate. Recently, Egypt and Libya have been in the news. A sermon about freedom, revolution or nonviolent, peaceful resistance would be appropriate.

BEHAVIOR

Drugs

I wrote and article published in the *San Francisco Chronicle* that expresses my views on drugs

Prizes for Pushers
By Robert Warren Cromey

Green Dolores Park slopes down from our twentieth street flat in San Francisco's Mission District. Kids play on the swings and romp in the sand. Gleeful play punishes the slides and the little merry-go-round. Joggers stride and bounce around the perimeters. The tennis and basketball courts burst with shouts and scores. On sunny days the terraces at the south end of the park become Dolores beach as hundreds of sunbathers languish on colorful towels and blankets.

Wife Ann jogs around the park. I often walk or just sit in the sun and watch the view of the silvery, sparkling city. At the corner of Church and Nineteenth Streets there is a J-Church trolley overpass. At almost any time of the day or night, young men are there to sell dope. Sometimes when I walk by I am approached with an offer to buy. I say, "No, thank you." and walk on by. The young man, often just a boy, turns and joins his friends.

Each time it happens I think of my old friend Barry Bloom, priest and house re-habber. He talks with his flat Boston accent and says, "The Chamber of Commerce should give those pushers a prize for their industry."

He says, "You know, Cromey, these kids are on to the American capitalist dream. They know the law of supply and demand. They know there is a demand for dope and they supply the stuff. They find a need and fill it." Lee Iacocca couldn't have said it better.

The pusher in Dolores Park knows the three basic laws for a successful business. Location, Location, Location. Nineteenth and Church has plenty of foot traffic, hundreds of cars pass by daily. The trolley bridge itself has views in all directions in case the police decide to raid. A buyer pulls up in her car and waves a green twenty. She is handed a baggie and off she goes down Church Street toward Eighteenth. Not fifteen seconds have passed. Zig Zigler, the world's greatest salesman, couldn't find a better location.

These entrepreneurs also know how to set prices to make a profit. They know how to do math in their heads quickly and accurately. They don't keep any books and thus keep endless numbers of deals, dealers and customers in their heads. They pay no taxes; that is the dream of every business owner. The business sections of large bookstores have dozens of books on how to avoid paying taxes.

These young men are real competitors. Sometimes six or seven are standing around the bridge together. When a likely buyer appears, they race each other on foot to be the first to make a sale. Last time I was in Macy's, no salesperson even looked my way. I had to go and find one to make my purchase.

They are experts in manipulating the legal system to their protection and benefit. They hire crack lawyers (pun intended) to keep them out of jail. Plea-bargaining is a well-hewn craft. They know the rules of evidence so they are seldom caught with any dope on their person. When police approach they toss their dope-laden baggies in the bushes.

They work very hard, are industrious. Morning, noon and night, seven days a week, no holidays or vacations, they ply their trade. These guys really know the value of hard work. One would think they had read Benjamin Franklin's *Poor Richard's Almanac*. They know that "the early bird catches the worm."

Many have families and take care of their aging parents. They buy food for their wives and children and feed members of their extended families. They should be honored for their family values.

They know how to protect their profits. They vigorously oppose the legalization of recreational drugs. Like good Republicans they don't want to be regulated by the government, their profits cut and, worst of all, have to pay taxes.

Since many of these young men are black or Latino, their livelihoods are seriously threatened by the decriminalization of drugs. Where will they go for jobs? Who will hire them? Where else in our American dream could they make such good money? Where in our economy would their business talents be put to good use and so well rewarded? How would they feed their families? Many would have to go on welfare. Putting them out of business would deprive the community of valuable cash and cost the government welfare money.

Just look at the economic value they provide to our communities. I shouldn't be so pessimistic. I'll bet Bank of America, IBM or Nordstrom would hire ex-dope peddlers who are such superb capitalists.

It really is time these hard working dope pushers be recognized and rewarded for their talents and abilities as business men in our community. Let's have the Commonwealth Club invite them to give a lunchtime lecture. Open the doors of the Pacific Union Club to these hard-working businessmen. Let the Chamber of Commerce help them take their rightful places among the business tycoons of our fair city and land.

Abortion

Abortion is a vexing issue. I don't like the idea of fetuses being destroyed. The physical and psychological pain many women suffer seems unbearable and unnecessary. The agony some women suffer at giving up a child for adoption has immediate and long term affects on many women. I told my daughters that if they ever got pregnant, we as a family would rally round and help them have the baby and help raise the child. I wish our society were financially and emotionally equipped to offer such help to all women who discover they have an unwanted pregnancy.

I am not a fan of the late Reverend Jerry Falwell, founder of the Moral Majority, but I heard him say on television that he and his church in Lynchburg, Virginia, rigorously opposed abortion but offered counseling and financial assistance to women who wanted to have their baby and either give it up to adoption or choose to keep the child. But the facts are that the poor do not have such resources available. Unwed mothers on welfare increasingly find the state and federal government unwilling to finance keeping alive a child without a father present.

The argument that abortion kills babies is correct and irrelevant. American society approves of killing. Americans overwhelmingly approve of capital punishment. That is killing. Every American who pays taxes participates in killing. Our government allows producers of weapons to sell to counties around the world. Those weapons kill people every minute of every hour of every day. Our government uses our tax money to wage war and support foreign wars around the world that kill people. "Thou shalt not kill" is a commandment that every taxpayer breaks as we pay our taxes. Adding state and federal funding for abortions is just another way we kill.

Sadly, I approve of abortion. Women have the right to choose what happens to their bodies. Women should have the right to abortion and poor women should receive financial help from the government to have safe abortions.

Capital Punishment

To remain inconsistent, I oppose capital punishment. My conversion from a warlike teenager to opposing the ultimate punishment came from viewing the movie, *Oxbow Incident*. Men were hung for a crime they did not commit. The movie ends when the innocent are dead and the real murderers are discovered. I remember being absolutely horrified at such an injustice. Certainly more of the poor are executed than the wealthy. Justice smiles more sweetly on the rich than on the poor. Blacks and Mexicans are executed far more than Whites. We hear it is cheaper to keep a person in prison for life than to finance years of appeals. There is no evidence that capital punishment is a deterrent to the perpetration of murder.

The Christian gospel calls for forgiveness and hope. We need to express compassion toward the families of victims of murder. We also need to express compassion for the killers. There can be no repentance and reconciliation if a person is executed. Life in prison without the possibility of parole gives a guilty person plenty of time to repent and think over the effect of the crime. Many, of course, regard life in prison as worse than capital punishment.

Christians also have this peculiar and radical notion that we must love our enemies. My enemy is a person who kills my child. I believe the killer needs to be convicted. Justice needs to be done. I hope I can love the killer enough not to kill him in vengeance and retaliation but allow her to be in prison until death comes in the course of time.

I do value the life of a person who makes it into the world more than a fetus who doesn't. I am willing to live with this ambiguity. Life is full of hard choices.

Sumptuary Law

Sumptuary laws attempt to control personal behavior or habits. These are drug use, prostitution and pornography. All kinds of laws are constructed to stop these activities, and none of them work. The attempts to outlaw them cost billions of dollars in tax money, and lives are lost in law enforcement attempts. Pornography has flourished under limited controls. Drug use and prostitution are banned, but they, too, flourish. My own view is that they all should be decriminalized and placed under government control.

We control legal drugs and alcohol successfully; there is no reason we cannot control the use of many hard drugs. Some countries have success in controlling the disease and degradation of prostitution. Puritanical America can't conceive of such liberality. Pornography exists under some controls. Any adult who wishes to read or view explicit sexual activity can do so. Yet the police, the religious right and other self-appointed protectors of our morals continue to trump up ways to harass the publishers and viewers of porno.

Porn

I do want to put in a good word for pornography. Yes, much pornography degrades women. Yes, it applauds sex for sex sake. Yes, it should not be available to children without parental consent. Viewing explicit sexual activity can also be fun, entertaining and a way to assist masturbatory fantasies. It also helps eroticize couples whose sexual juice has diminished and who want to use videos in their foreplay. My late friend, the pornographer, made videos of men having sex with other men. He also contributed financially to Trinity Church. Clearly he has a self-interest in finding value in porno. He used to say he thought of lonely gay men in small towns in Middle America who used his videos for masturbation and achieve some self-satisfaction, physical relief and pleasure. Chances of meeting gay men in small towns are extremely limited and often risky.

Video sex can give comfort and sensual relief. Not a bad rationalization. It is on a better level than the notion that porno should be banned because it may lead some to violence. I suspect action, horror and adventure movies and television shows lead more youngsters to violence than sex videos do. My motto for movies and television is more sex and less violence.

Porno videos and books minister to our voyeuristic and fantasy needs. Seeing nudity and active sex are concrete images about being open, free, loose and relaxed. We all yearn for such ways of being, but society's constraints rightly prevent us from acting out on the bus or in church. Deep down we wish we could act with such abandon. Pornography is a symbol of behavior that most of us can never achieve.

In addition, explicitly sexual videos are opportunities to see naked bodies of beautiful men and women. Another best-kept secret is that men and women enjoy looking at beautiful, naked people. There are few places or arenas where such viewing is available.

Porno is a multi-billion dollar business in this country. There is no way laws are going to stop the dissemination of sexually explicit books and videos. There will always be pornography. There will always be vigorous opposition to it. I suppose that is the American way of life and capitalism.

Two excellent books that give a positive view of pornography are:

Talk Dirty to Me, An Intimate Philosophy of Sex, by Sallie Tisdale, Doubleday, 1994 (I sent a copy to each of my adult daughters.)

Bound and Gagged by Laura Kipnis, Grove Press, 1996

Prostitution

Prostitution will always be with us. "Find a need and fill it" is a capitalist motto. Prostitutes will always have a market. Some men are just horny, some like the adventure of being with a whore, some like the dangers, some enjoy the anonymity, some are needy, and some are randy. Certainly prostitution degrades those women who are forced into the profession. It is a terrible sin to push young girls into the racket. Yet many women go into the work because they choose to make money by selling their bodies rather than waiting tables and working in an office.

The only prostitute I ever talked to about the profession was a young woman who came to me for therapy in my days as a marriage and family counselor. The issue was should she tell the man she lives with that she takes clients for sex during the day. The question was truth telling. It was not should she or should she not be a prostitute. She was a slim, sweet, rather plain-of-face woman of about thirty-two. She told me that she had several regular male customers. She went to them about once a week, stayed and hour or two, had oral sex and intercourse, chatted amiably then dressed, took her money and returned home or went to another customer. She knew exactly what she was doing. She was not forced to have sex for money. Her activity is illegal. She enjoyed it. She told me she had no intention of stopping.

There are untold numbers of women who are prostitutes for some period in their lives. These are different from the hookers on the street corner who risk life and limb from the johns. They also may be getting and passing along dread diseases to the men they have sex with. But prostitution will always be with us.

I truly believe we should decriminalize the trade, register sex workers, have them examined regularly for health problems and let them ply their trade. We can also tax them. Hookers and capitalists are against such regulation. Both want little government involvement in their lives and do not want to pay taxes.

Such regulation would not discourage hooking. Some women would play the game and register. Some would not. Certainly the high-class hookers who take care of rich, traveling men prefer private enterprise.

Prostitution can be an honorable profession. It is a way for women to have control over their bodies and a way they earn a living.

Prohibition

Prohibition, television at its finest is a three-part program produced by Ken Burns on PBS. We see that the U.S. Government was pressured into passing the 18th amendment to the Constitution, which made alcohol illegal. The television program shows and tells us how it came about, what were the consequences and how it was repealed. It is told vividly and dramatically using old still pictures, movies and detailed narratives to bring the viewer into the very times it was all happening. The clothes, the cars, the characters, the buildings, the farms, the small towns and the big cities of our vast country draw us into other eras.

The "drys" were determined to end the drinking of alcohol as the way to stop drunkenness, broken homes, abuse of women and children, job loss, production interruption and alcoholism. The "wets" did not want laws passed controlling their behavior and right to drink. They also made fortunes making beer and whiskey as well as producing jobs for distillers, barrel makers, glassmakers, brewers, and farmers growing corn and grain. The taxes helped the government.

The rigid determination and organization of the "drys" won out, and the 18th Amendment was passed into law in 1919. The Protestant churches supported the amendment. Only the Episcopalians and Lutherans refrained. The intended consequences were that there was a drop in alcohol consumption and alcoholism. Breweries and distillers and saloons closed down.

The unintended consequences sprang into life almost immediately. Speakeasies, scofflaws and illegal importing and smuggling of alcohol into the country began at once. Illegal booze made some people sick, blind and dead. Gangsters using sophisticated business methods produced whiskey and beer and distributed it to the customers who lined up to drink. Otherwise law-abiding citizens who wanted to drink felt bad but went ahead buying and drinking illegal booze.

The third part of the series reports the movement toward and the final repeal of the 18th amendment by the 21st Amendment in 1933. This finale is made dramatic with film and audio footage of the nomination and election of Franklin Delano Roosevelt as President of the United States. He opposed the 18th amendment.

This wonderful television series raises the issues of attempts to control people's behavior and of single-minded rigidity and pressure politics.

Americans today want most drugs to be illegal, such as marijuana, cocaine, LSD and other so-called recreational drugs. As a result, there is a vast illegal drug trade throughout the United States. Drugs are easily available in most high schools and colleges, places of business and even in prisons. Jails bulge with men and women serving sentences for possession and use of even the least harmful drugs. Misinformation is given to children hoping they will refrain from drug use. The kids regard these classes as a joke. Illegal drugs are a multi-billion-dollar industry in this country.

In Sum

Prostitution is outlawed almost everywhere and flourishes all over the place. Where there is demand there is supply. It too is a multi-billion-dollar that goes untaxed. Women continue to be demeaned, injured and exploited by corrupt police as well as by their pimps and customers.

The rigidity of the National Rifle Association's (NRA) opposition to any controls means that guns are easily available to youngsters, the mentally and emotionally disturbed and people in a rage for vengeance. City teen gangs find all the guns they want. Many members of the NRA would like more flexibility about some gun control, but the leaders at the top rigidly oppose any gun control.

Prohibition taught us that Americans must be aware that some groups in our country try to control our behavior and our thinking. They are not open to serious discussion or debate. They are only interested in getting their way. Of course that is a natural tendency in all of us. We all want our own way.

I am a firm believer in democracy, freedom of speech and the interchange of ideas. We must always be aware of our own tendencies and of those who want to control us and our behavior and values.

Alcohol and Behavior

Twas a woman who drove me to drink. I never had the courtesy to thank her.

—W.C. Fields

I am a drinker. I enjoy a martini, very cold, straight up with an olive—gin not vodka. When a waiter asks me if I want a vodka martini, I put on my snooty routine and reply, "Had I wanted potato soup, I'd have asked for it." Sometimes a bartender does not listen to my order and asks if I want a lemon twist? I reply in mock high dudgeon, "No twist please, had I wanted a fruit salad I'd have requested it." I like a Manhattan, straight up with a cherry. The brand of bourbon and red vermouth doesn't seem to matter. The more expensive, richer whiskeys make the drink too sweet and rich for my taste; I also like a good single malt scotch on the rocks. Yes, I know "real men" drink it neat. Why spoil a good whiskey with ice, you ask? I don't care; I like it on the rocks. Glenlivet is right for me. The better, richer, darker, smokier scotches must be okay, but I don't like them much. I like a beer with Indian food. I like red and white wine and am not fussy about palates, aftertastes, tannins, fruitiness, brands and price. Our table wines are Fetzer.

I like to tell our guests that, if they want a fine wine for dinner, they had best bring what they like, and we will serve it. Otherwise you drink the rotgut we provide. I remember that Mary likes Pinot Grigio, and Susan likes white. Michael and Rob like single malt neat. Ann likes Calistoga. Edwin and Adam like vodka, and Pam likes white wine with a cube in it. That is the extent of my bartender's memory.

I sometimes wonder if I am an alcoholic or am I just an enjoyer of booze? For many years, especially when I was still *rectoring*, I enjoyed cocktail time—a martini or Manhattan while sitting in my big chair, reading a magazine or something light and just relaxing and enjoying the buzz and comfort of a drink at that time of day. I would then prepare dinner and dine with Ann when she got up from her post school day nap. I sometimes nipped a second drink in the kitchen or had a glass of wine while finishing the dinner preparation. At dinner we had a half bottle of wine between us but I drank most of it.

Back a few years when we were having a typical church row over something, one member of the church alleged I was an alcoholic. The parish secretary, a twelve stepper and recovering alcoholic, replied, "I have never seen Robert drunk."

Ann and I would talk about my drinking. She did not like it that I drank. A former Mormon, you know. We talked about health problems and even the benefits of alcohol consumption. Ann reads lots of health magazines and the opinion of the month about drinking changes virtually every month with each new health letter.

A little alcohol is good for you. All alcohol is bad for you. Red wine is better than white. White is better than red. People who drink moderately live longer. People that don't drink at all live longer—Seventh Day Adventists and Mormons, for instance. So we would go round and round. AA suggests ninety meetings in ninety days. If you can go the distance, you are probably not an alcoholic. I never tried it, and I don't want to.

I did decide I was not necessarily interested in living to a ripe old age. I want to have a good time while I am alive. Part of a good time is drinking. So Ann and I would chat about my drinking from time to time.

Then one day I remembered reading about *focus on behavior.* This is a good technique when evaluating an employee. I realized the drinking is not the problem; the behavior is the problem. I asked Ann to focus on the behavior that I presented, not on the value of drink itself. "Tell me what I do and how I behave when I drink that annoys you." Ann said, "When you drink, you get critical, short and sometimes slur your speech." So I began to watch that behavior of mine after I had a few drinks. Sure enough I noticed I became easily annoyed, impatient and indeed did slur my speech.

Now that was behavior in myself that I did not like. I did not like that it hurt Ann and interfered with my communicating verbally. I knew I wanted to change the behavior. To change the behavior I cut way back on my cocktails and drinking in general. I stopped drinking cocktails, substituted a glass of wine or a beer while preparing dinner and had some wine with dinner.

I found that indeed my behavior changed when I curbed the drinking. I also slept better at night and felt better in the mornings. I am able to read for a couple of hours in the evening instead of going to bed very early.

I have a cocktail when we go out to dinner and very occasionally have one at home. I do not go to bars. The change in my habits of drinking have modified my behavior and improved our already wonderful relationship.

This way of evaluating drinking and behavior may not work for everybody. So far, it works for us and for me.

Giving Relief I

Maureen was in love with me. She'd call my answering machine just to hear my voice. She came to my groups just to be near me. She was short, had curly blondish hair, blue eyes, a chubby figure and a dark red hemangioma over the right side of her face. She was aggressive, funny, pushy, obnoxious, tender and vulnerable. In spite of her disfigured face she had men friends and a couple of husbands and live-in lovers over the years.

Before she accepted the fact that she was different-looking from other people, she tried cosmetics, bleaches and many quack methods to remove the red stain from the side of her face. Then she said she just accepted the fact one day. She used to say, "What you see is what you get," but of course her stain obsessed her. She talked about it a lot and worked in our group therapy sessions on her grief and sadness about her face. She never blamed her parents, God or anyone, but it was always with her. She married and had two daughters. Raised the children and divorced.

When I met her, she was a masseuse with her own private practice. She had a studio and did house and hotel calls. She always seemed to have money, paid her own way and drank a bit. Sometimes she called on the phone and rambled on about her unhappiness just to talk with me.

She told me she was not a prostitute, but that from time to time she would *give relief*. When she massaged men, sometimes they got an erection. She would masturbate them or give them blowjobs. She described the activity in a very business-like and objective manner. It was just something she did as part of the job. It never seemed like a big deal to her. I never heard she got arrested. She usually only gave relief when the client requested that service. Knowing Maureen, she probably suggested it when she saw the man getting really hot. It was certainly one way to calm a man down.

She was always after me to give me a massage. I finally relented. She did not use oil, only her hands rubbing my body. It was not unpleasant. But it was a first for me and I would have preferred fragrant oil. I did not get an erection; she made no sexual move toward me. It was not the best massage I ever had. I'll confess that I was a little leery of Maureen's intention, but there was no hint of ulterior motive.

One day in the fall of 1979, I got a call from Maureen. I had not heard from her in a long time as I had been out of the country for a year. She was weeping and very upset. She asked if she could come and see me. When she arrived, she blurted out that her friend, Peter, had just been murdered. He was a popular California politician shot in his office. I of course knew about the shootings and was as shocked and bewildered as we all were at that time.

"I used to give Peter massages. He would come to my studio. Sometimes I would give him relief. I loved him. He is a married man. There is no one I can talk to about this. Oh, I am so sad and shocked," Maureen sputtered through her tears.

She stayed in my office for an hour or so, crying, telling stories, being ashamed, grateful, happy, miserable, even saying she'd get through it all, but she would miss him. After a while she seemed relieved and left.

I saw her a couple of times for coffee or a drink. A former Roman Catholic, she hated all churches and never came to Trinity. She married a retired firefighter and later separated from him.

In 2005, after I had already retired, Maureen's daughter asked me to come to the hospital to visit Maureen, who was in a coma and dying. I did come to her bedside, talked with her and told her who I was, hoping that the sound of my voice might penetrate the gloom of her darkened mind. I hope it did. Her bubbly, feisty life with the undercurrent of scarred sadness was relieved by death soon after my visit.

Giving Relief II

In September of 1969, my friend and mentor, Bishop James Albert Pike, died in the desert while traveling in Israel. He was researching Christian origins. His wife Diane accompanied him as they talked with historians and theologians. Through a series of mishaps and poor judgment the couple got lost as they drove. Diane went looking for help, Pike abandoned the car, fell off a cliff and died. We were shocked and saddened by the news.

Pike had been the very prominent Bishop of the Diocese of California for eight years. He resigned, because his womanizing and non-traditional theological views caused criticism and

controversy. I was vicar of St. Aidan's Church in San Francisco.
I got a telephone call from a sobbing woman. She was socially
prominent and an active Episcopalian. I have forgotten her
name these forty plus years later. I will call her Nancy. She
asked if she could come and see me. Entering my study, she sat
quickly and spewed out her story. Nancy was one of the many
women with whom Pike had had affairs. She had been in love
with him and knew she could never marry him. She also knew
Pike had any number of women lovers.

Nancy wanted to see me as she felt she had no one else to
talk with about her grief. She knew that I had been a member
of the Bishop's staff and a confidant. She was in her fifties—
tall, slender and worldly wise. Her hair was perfect and only
slightly graying. Her blue eyes shone over a cobalt silk dress.
Nancy dared not tell her husband, friends or clergy. She knew
that I could keep a secret and that I knew that Pike had had
affairs. She wept as she recounted their relationship in hotel
and motel rooms when he was traveling and occasionally in
her home when her husband was away. Nancy admitted that
she "sat at his feet" when he lectured, preached and presided at
meetings. If anyone suspected her infatuation and adultery, she
was fearful of losing her husband, reputation and position on
the church boards where she was prominent and powerful.

I mostly listened and let her find relief in airing her pain
and grief. We stayed together for an hour or so. Nancy stood
up, wiped her eyes and nose, gave me a quick hug and left. I
never saw her again.

Take a Day Off From Retirement

The cliché is so true: I am so busy in retirement; I wonder how
I got any work done when I was employed. For me these past
ten years have been delightfully busy with traveling, reading,
exercising and occasional preaching. Then there is writing,
entertaining and shopping and cooking, which I have always
done in my marriage to Ann. The last twenty years of my now
fifty-four-year ministry was at Trinity Church, San Francisco,
a lively downtown inner-city parish.

After a couple of years of not working, I discovered I was too occupied to enjoy my new life. I was running, to-ing and fro-ing, lurching from event to event—appointments, examinations, classes and lunches. I realized I was not retired; I was just busy. After a hard look at how I was spending my time, I decided to take a day off from my retirement. One day a week I make no medical appointments, lunch or dinner dates, shopping or library trips. I take a day of rest. Sound familiar?

"Remember that thou keep holy the Sabbath Day." I used to keep Sunday as a holy day by working at church, preaching, teaching, leading youth group meeting with the vestry and celebrating Eucharist. It certainly was not a day of rest. While an active priest, I took my day off, but that was not a day of rest. Shopping, cooking, exercising, reading and having to do with my work—attending to the house and yard and washing the car took up my day off.

Orthodox Jews keep the Sabbath as a day of no work. They go to great lengths to avoid work of any kind. No cooking, no traveling in a vehicle, no turning on or off lights, no dropping in at the office. Sex between spouses is encouraged. In this time of 24/7 and type A personalities, we need to heed the wisdom of the Jews. Our bodies and souls need rest, quiet—a restoration to holiness and sanity. Some Mormons also hold Sunday as a day of worship and quiet. No cooking, no business and even the children are excused from homework.

Taking a day off from work or retirement is difficult for the formerly busy parish priest. In fact we clergy pride ourselves on being busy. That notion smacks a bit of justification by works. It often carries over into retirement. Not me. In addition to taking a day off from retirement, I schedule only one or two major activities a day. I attend a weekly vigil for peace. It is near the library where I make a weekly stop for books and DVDs. That's it for that day.

Yet it is important to note that people are different. We have different paces and styles. Traveling is a good example. My wife, Ann, and many of my friends like to get to London or Paris and visit as many museums, grand houses, gardens, castles, ruins, plays and churches as possible. They go from breakfast to bedtime, stopping only for lunch and dinner. Others are more like me. Up in the morning, I go off to the café for coffee, croissant and some fruit. I get the English edition of the *Herald Tribune*, read for an hour, do the crossword puzzle and jaunt off to a museum to join my wife for an hour and then a bite of lunch.

She goes on to other venues while I wander back to our hotel or apartment for a nap and some reading. I love to shop and cook in foreign climes so I do that so dinner is ready when Ann returns. We enjoy good restaurants and often go out to eat. Sometimes we go to the theater, but more often we read and go to bed early. I have any number of friends who have similar lazy ways of touring. I used to feel guilty that I did not get more out of my travel dollars. I now am clear that I travel the way I do, not the way I don't. We are all different in the way we travel and choose to lead our lives.

We Anglicans don't have rules hovering over us to order our lives, travel, work or retirement. We have the enormous freedom of choosing our own path and program. The bad thing is that we often are in disarray about our schedules. The good thing is that we have the freedom to order our own lives. We can learn from the Jews and the Mormons, the Benedictines and Franciscans and spiritual directors who have sprung up among us. But finally it is up to us to order and regulate our lives for enjoyment and refreshment.

The old story is that God rested on the seventh day. The ancients knew that their bodies needed rest from toil in order to be creative and productive during the rest of the week. Working or retired, we Americans, clergy and lay, need to learn to rest, keep quiet, listen to music, enjoy nature and feel the pulsing of our bodies. So take a day off from retirement.

ET CETERA

Reflections of an Amateur Economist

The nation is in the biggest financial crisis since the great depression and fall of the stock market in 1929. The mortgage industry has collapsed causing the fall of the stock market. Loans are hard to get. The government is trying to bail out failing financial institutions. "Socialism for the rich" is what the late John Henry Galbraith has called it. Big business wants no control so it can play ball in free market capitalism. But when big business gets in trouble, it wants the government to help it out of the difficulties it has gotten itself into.

We are okay as we are both retired. The Church Pension Fund has a ten-billion-dollar portfolio; so I expect my monthly check is okay. So far Social Security is stable. Ann's pension is in stocks and bonds; so that may waiver a bit, but we are okay. I suspect that most Americans and we will ride this out without undue suffering. At least that is my fondest hope.

This crisis goes to the root of human nature. Many people believe that we are born pure and innocent then are damaged and corrupted by the wicked world. My belief is that human nature is deeply flawed to begin with. We are born with a basic inclination to self-preservation, which never really leaves us. We all want to do good, but we don't do it. We all want to avoid doing bad things, but we do them anyway. We will do anything to protect and enhance our self-interest. To put it another way, we are radically imperfect.

But there is the other side of human nature. At the same time we are imperfect, we have a drive toward love and compassion. These two sides of our nature are in constant tension. In raising children we adore our children, and their behavior causes us to be angry and punishing. We fall wildly in love with our partners, but we can be hostile, mean and unfaithful. We want to be honest and profitable in our businesses, yet we lie, cheat and steal sometimes. The good and the bad are there in us all the time. The truly mature human being knows about these warring tendencies and is in control of them.

I think the mortgage brokers, stock brokers and government employees are no better or worse than the rest of us. They are a combination of good and evil. They love their spouses and children. Many enjoy their work and want to make money to live well and be responsible citizens. Then greed, the desire for a little or a lot more comes into play. Temptation comes, and risks become exciting; there is even the possibility of great wealth. Sometimes it pays off, and lots of money is made. This will always happen for a few people. The risks are worth it.

When I make lots of money then I can give lots of it away. That is true, and many wealthy people do just that. Some don't.

Free market capitalism doesn't work, because it does not take into account the fact that people are as bad as they are good. People are as greedy as they are generous. Destroying competition, evading taxes, hostile takeovers and endangering and underpaying workers are some of the evils of capitalism. Free-market capitalism always leaves a good number of people at the bottom of the economic heap—hungry, homeless, sick and degraded.

Controlled capitalism is the system we have in the United States now. Congress had done many things to control rampant runaway capitalism and its abuses. They have allowed labor unions to exist to demand better working conditions and pay for employees. Until recently there was strong legislation in place to control some of the abuses of people playing the stock market. The government controls farm, energy and communication policies.

Only the government is big and strong enough to assure that all Americans have adequate medical care. Capitalism has failed in providing medical care to millions of American men, women and children. The fear of "socialized medicine" has given pause to real comprehensive medical care for us all. I think the government must get more deeply involved to assure widespread medical care for all.

Our business and political leaders are imperfect, a combination of good and bad. They are doing their best in a difficult and complex financial world. They have trouble keeping their allegiances straight. What is good for the country, the economy, the party, the world, the ecology and their families?

We love a simple-minded blame game. It is the Republicans, the Democrats, the Unions who are to blame is the usual way. A more realistic way is to get past the blame game to what is the best way to move forward, make changes and keep our country healthy. We need an attitude of trust that in getting the facts and solutions we need, we can live comfortably in a world where human being are imperfect and good at the same time.

The Murder of Bin Laden

I got an email from my granddaughter, Mary Charlotte, asking me what I thought of the killing of Osama bin Laden. I was flattered that she would be interested in my opinion.

I was surprised by my own lack of gladness at the news of Bin Laden's killing. I was sad for the American people who want vengeance before justice. I was sad for the relatives of the victims of the horror of the 9/11 atrocities. I was sad that the President said justice had been done when he announced bin Laden was disposed of.

Many in our country think an eye for an eye is proper revenge. Mary Charlotte quoted, "An eye for an eye makes the whole world blind." We are blind to why we are so hated in many parts of the world. Our quest for oil, our profits from trade with poor countries, our support for tyrannical governments, our support for slavery and our oppression of women makes us appear callous, vicious and oblivious to the poor and the needy. Yes, we will generously give money and aid to victims of famines, hurricane, earthquakes and volcanoes. However, our government and big business do little to alleviate the underlying social, political and economic problems that cause hunger, poverty and lack of education, water and medical care to poor people around the world.

Putting Bin Laden on trial would have brought to surface the radical hatred and profound reasons why people hate our country and its policies. Perhaps that is why he was not taken a prisoner but killed by U.S. bullets. In any case, the American system of trial by jury—facing the consequences of causing of the deaths of so many people and facing life in prison— would have been a far more just yet painful punishment for his invidious and admitted crimes.

Singing

On Thursday, August 26, 2010, I sent this letter to a *San Francisco Chronicle* columnist, Jon Carroll who had written about singing.

> Your column referring to singing reminded me how I, too, love to sing. I can carry a tune and stay on pitch. I sing in the car, walking along and even when I swimming, sing in my head.
>
> I get to sing regularly and loudly as I go to church on Sundays, one of the few venues for corporate singing in our time. I suspect some people sing the *Star Spangled Banner* when they go to baseball games. A few people who are really good singers join choral groups, which are expensive and rigorous. There is not much singing in barrooms anymore.

Once I lost a bet and had to go to a Grateful Dead Concert and was very impressed how many people sang along with the late Jerry and the boys. Because there were no words displayed anywhere, I was sentenced to listen. At Christmastime lots of people go caroling; some go to sing-a-long Messiahs, and churches are pretty full of singers at that time of year.

John Wesley, the founder of the Methodist Church, had his congregations sing a couple of rousing hymns to shake off the dust of the world, open their throats and hearts and deepen their breathing to prepare for the hearing the Word.

One banker member of Trinity Episcopal, where I was rector for twenty years said, "I sing in the choir, because I need a good shout at least once a week."

After writing that letter I thought some more about singing. My Dad used to sing to my brother and me. The terrible anti-Semitic *O Sheeny Levi* was one I can remember. He sang it with humor and a sense of fun. I think back on it with embarrassment. He and my mother sang nursery rhymes and Christmas and other hymns. My mother was good enough to be a choir member in Dad's churches. She sang solos, such as *Oh Promise Me, God So Loved the World,* and, at home, *Always* and other popular songs of her day.

As a boy soprano, I sang, *Joseph Tender, Joseph Mild,* and *Help Me Rock this Babe Divine.* My voice broke, and I am sure few could hear me. It was at a Christmas Eve service at Church of the Redeemer, Astoria, Queens, New York, in the early 1940s. I was in the choir as was my mother. We had rehearsals one night a week and sang on Sundays. Tom Mazza was the organist and choirmaster.

In the '40s, at P.S. 5, Queens, I took some singing lessons, mostly breathing instruction. I dropped out. At St. Paul's School we sang one hymn every morning before classes began. In seminary we had singing and chanting lessons as a student body and some individual training, and we sang and chanted

Morning Prayer, Eucharist and Evensong every day while in class. After that, I sang in church almost every Sunday of my life to this day.

In the '50s I sang to my children when they were small, often when driving in the car. I recall *The Keeper of the Eddystone Light:*

My father was the keeper of the Eddystone light
And he slept with a mermaid one fine night
Out of this union there came three
A porpoise and a porgy and the other was me!

I can remember. *Sweet Betsey From Pike*, a Burl Ives Song, I think.

Oh, do you remember Sweet Betsey from Pike
Who crossed the wide prairie with her lover Ike?
With two yoke of oxen, a big yellow dog,
A tall Shanghai rooster, and one spotted hog.
Hoodle dang, fol-de-dye do,
hoodle dang, fol-de day.

Singing was such a regular part of church life and my own life that I never thought about it very much. I never felt comfortable chanting the priest's part of the Mass so I seldom if ever did. I'd say the parts instead. I certainly hate the chanting in general in church and hate it even more when the clergy do it badly.

Singing is just a natural part of my life, and I enjoy singing whenever I do it. Now in my eighties, I notice my voice is not very strong, and I lose pitch sometimes.

Favorite hymns are *Jesus Christ is Risen Today; The Strife is O'er, the Battle is Done; I Want to Walk as a Child of the Light; Immortal, Invisible, God Only Wise; Hark! The Herald Angels Sing and Silent Night*, among others.

OBITUARIES

The Reverend Edward Joseph Berey
May 14, 1930 - December 24, 2010

Edward was in the General Theological Seminary, New York City, class of 1956. He was in classes with me and seemed distant, reserved, a bit wise-ass and hostile. My then wife, Lillian, took a liking to him and invited him to dinner with us. We became acquainted and quite good friends for the rest of the time in seminary and afterward. I found we laughed and gossiped at all the same things.

Ed had been in Military Intelligence in the U.S. Army during the Korean War and came to seminary afterward. We were ordained together on June 17, 1956, by Horace Donegan, Bishop of New York, who gave Ed a white stole as Ed did not own one.

Ed became a member of the church when he had been placed in an Episcopal orphanage, as his parents were not able physically and financially to care for him although they were both alive. He went on to Guilford College in North Carolina. He told me he felt bad that his family left him in the home.

After ordination Edward was sent to a small church in Tuxedo, New York, where he had various troubles and excommunicated his senior warden. Ed had a quick temper and judgmental style. He pulled rank when pastoral care was needed. The Bishop had to intervene. Lillian and our daughters, Leigh and Sarah, visited Ed in Tuxedo. He was the godfather to our second child, Sarah, born in 1958. He kept in touch and we with him by telephone in those days.

Ed's second job was as an assistant in a parish on Staten Island. He was unhappy there, as he did not get along with his boss who was rector of the parish.

When Edward's mother died in the late fifties, he asked me to do the funeral service for her. I was honored to do so.

Ed soon moved on to Seattle where he became head of camps for the diocese. He seemed to enjoy his work there. He married a woman named Sharon, and they had a daughter, Helen. After the divorce she married Jim Michel who has since died.

According to Ed, his wife's parents did not approve of him, partly because of his dark, middle-European skin. They accused him of being of another race. When Ed and his wife had problems, she went to stay with her parents. When Helen and the parents moved to have the marriage dissolved, Ed was forbidden to see Helen. Ed resented that the Bishop there never helped him in his marital problems and allowed these rich Episcopalians to so manipulate things that he lost contact with his daughter. Please, dear reader, I have only Ed's side of the story, and it was many yeas ago that I heard it. Ed, like many—and me—have trouble with authority and lash out against it when we feel wronged.

I had moved to San Francisco in 1962. Ed visited us and stayed with us for several weeks. During that time I put his name in to be rector of Church of St. John the Evangelist here in the city. He got the job and was supposed to work together with three other churches and me to help those weak churches grow. Ed and I had conflicts, as he was not cooperative, as I saw it, in our joint efforts. He said he did not have to follow us as he was a rector and could stand alone.

Several of the other clergy and I became very active and public in the civil rights movement. We picketed auto agencies and hotels that discriminated against minorities. Ed did not join us. He wanted to be separate from our ministry and had a secretive quality of not wanting to be public with his opinions. I am sure he was for civil rights for all, but he did not want to join our efforts. We saw each other socially and played tennis from time to time. He was much better at it than I was.

Ed stayed at St. John's for a few years, married Patricia Penn and moved to Marin. He became involved with the Federal poverty program in that county. We did not speak or have contact for a decade. He and Patricia divorced. He was very devoted to his daughters, Rachael and Alisandra. He often spoke wistfully of Helen.

Edward and I met up at a clergy conference, laughed at each other and became friends again. We saw each other from time to time in Marin or in San Francisco for lunch. Later he met Jill. They married in the 1980s, and I was invited to perform the ceremony, which I did in Bolinas, California. I was married to Ann by then, and she accompanied me to the wedding. Soon Jill and Edward had Adam, and he was thrilled to be a proud father at fifty years old.

Again I saw Ed from time to time. I had become the rector of Trinity, San Francisco, in 1981. Ed and Jill divorced, but Ed was still anxious to be a good, divorced Dad and told me he did all he could to stay in contact with Adam. I always admired his devotion to his children.

Ed took Episcopal services when clergy were on vacation and wanted a weekend off. He was living in Cotati when I last saw him.

He told me that he had developed prostate cancer and was coming to the city to the Veteran's Hospital for treatments. He also went for dental treatment at the University of the Pacific clinic on Webster Street. We met rather regularly for a while over lunch when he came to the City. He had another woman friend, who lived in the northwest, and she came to see him in Cotati. German I think.

He wrote for a local paper, a humor column called *Elderberry*, which was quite wry and delightful. He has a real talent for words and observing the absurdity of life.

Our last and final falling out was in December of 2006. It was the fiftieth anniversary of our ordination as priests. I was planning to celebrate Eucharist and preach on December 17, 2006, a Sunday. I invited Ed to come to the service, read the gospel and assist at the service. He said he did not want to be only a deacon. I wanted him to do both, as I had been rector for twenty years and retired from there for four. No one in the parish knew Edward. He felt diminished and cut off all contact with me.

On December 21, 2010, I heard from Rachel that Edward had terminal lung cancer and was dying in a skilled nursing facility in Marin County.

Ed was charming and had a good sense of humor. He used to tease that he was the only Hungarian priest in the Episcopal Church. His parents' origins were Hungarian. He had black hair, dark eyes and an olive complexion. He was slender, wiry and physically strong.

He certainly could charm and had no trouble winning women. He was the flirt of flirts. His act with a waitress was annoying and delightful. He would ask endless questions about the menu, ask what she liked best and pulled delaying tactics that annoyed Adam and me once when we dined together.

Edward enjoyed being a pastor and cared for his parishioners and those committed to his charge. He was liberal on social issues

He was argumentative and relentless in discussion and had trouble letting go of a subject if he thought he was right. He got in trouble for driving under the influence of alcohol but was a moderate drinker when last I saw him.

He was very much an individual and walked to the beat of a different drummer. He distrusted bishops and church structure He was bitter toward the church, as he got almost no pension. Because he worked as a supply priest, the local churches paid him a fee but did not pay into the Church Pension Fund. So although he worked for the church, he received few benefits. I don't blame him for his attitude toward the church.

One tactic that used to drive me nuts was "Cromey why don't you write the Bishop..." about whatever issue he wanted to bring up. "Cromey, why don't you write to the *Chronicle* about...?

He also was a blamer. Most often when he spoke to me about problems he was having, it was because the other person did something wrong. I do not remember him ever taking responsibility for anything that ever happened to him. I never heard what happened to end his marriages in any detail, but it was always because the woman did something wrong.

I always liked Ed. I know he liked and cared for me and was interested in my work. He was not easy to be with, and I often felt myself on the defensive with him. I think his ministry with the poverty program and his work with street kids in Marin was his most satisfying job. He was very proud of that work and spoke of it often. I also know he was immensely proud of his children and really loved and cared for them.

Some further thoughts. Frankly, I have been rather haunted about Ed in the last few days. Perhaps I should have tried to reach him—to kiss and make up. How devastating it must have been for Edward to have been in an orphanage knowing his parents were alive. He alluded to the fact about that experience but not about the emotional devastation it must have caused him. I wonder if he was ridiculed by the other children, who had no parents and teased Edward that he had parents but they put him in the home. How much he must have feared rejection but often seemed to court it. Part of why he became a priest was because the orphanage was an Episcopal institution. I believe the orphanage school and or the church helped put Edward through college. Then he felt the church had rejected him. These are the thoughts that run through my mind these past days.

Bishop Pike
February 14, 1913 - September 1969

The Strange and Wonderful Witness of Bishop James Pike.[4]

Forty years ago, come September, Bishop James A. Pike died in the Judean desert. It happened while The Episcopal Church was in the midst of the Special Convention being held in South Bend, Indiana. At that meeting the House of Bishops would have taken formal notice to certify that Bishop Pike had abandoned "the communion of this Church." By the time he died Bishop Pike had become a confounding presence for everyone liberal and conservative. (photo to right from Wikipedia article on James Pike.)

William Stringfellow and Anthony Towne, in *The Death and Life of Bishop Pike*, noted that

> The day when Bishop Pike was missing in the Holy Land coincided with a general convention of the Episcopal Church held at Notre Dame University. A newspaperman tells me that he noted no prayer was said at the convention when the report of Pike being lost first reached South Bend. The journalist asked a dignitary—"Can't you guys even pray for Pike?" "We haven't had a chance to consult about it," was the reply. At the next session, my informant reports, there was a prayer - a *composite* prayer, he called it, mentioning in the same breath Bishop Pike and Ho Chi Minh. As the reporter concluded: "They prayed for all their enemies, all together." (p.435)

---

4 Written by Mark Harris, Episcopal Priest of Delaware, August 16, 2009, http://anglicanfuture.blogspot.com

When his death was finally confirmed, the House of Bishops unanimously adopted the following resolution, Stringfellow and Towne wrote,

> The death to self in Christ was neither doctrinal abstraction or theological jargon for James Pike. He died in such a way before his death in Judea. He died to authority, celebrity, the opinions of others, publicity, status, dependence upon Mama, indulgences in alcohol and tobacco, family and children, marriage and marriages, promiscuity, scholarly ambition, the lawyer's profession, political opportunity, Olympian discourses, forensic agility, controversy, denigration, injustice, religion, the need to justify himself.

> By the time Bishop Pike reached the wilderness in Judea, he had died in Christ. What, then, happened there was not so much a death as a birth. In the past few weeks I have been reading a trilogy of novels by Philip K. Dick, the so-called VALIS trilogy - Consisting of VALIS, The Divine Invasion, and The Transmigration of Timothy Archer. The last of these, The Transmigration of Timothy Archer is closely based on the life of Bishop Pike and reaches much the same conclusion regarding what really happened to him. Philip Dick writes, (remember Tim is Bishop Pike) "It was Tim who came back out of compassion." "That's right...He sought wisdom, the Holy Wisdom of God and when he got there and the Presence entered him, he realized that it was not wisdom that he wanted, but compassion.... he already had wisdom but it hadn't done him or anyone else any good." (p. 241, Vintage Book edition)

It turns out that Philip Dick knew Bishop Pike. According to the Wikipedia article on Pike he officiated at Dick's wedding to Nancy Hackett in 1966, so the wheel goes round and round. I was put on to this trilogy by Matthew, our son, who I in turn provoked to reading Philip Dick's other novels. He sent me the trilogy in particular because of *The Divine Invasion.* a book by Dick that grew from his having a cluster of profoundly psychological and spiritual visions. So here we are in Episcopal /Anglican land, forty years after Bishop Pike's death and we are still struggling with all the same issues. The struggle to be inclusive continues, the push back with charges of heresy is always there, the pilgrimages we are all on continue.

Bishop Pike at the end believed he had to give up the church in order to keep up the struggle to be authentic to his pilgrimage. His needs for autonomy in his pilgrimage were met by other means. He died still a bishop in the church.

Pike: Thoughts and Reflections from Pike's Friends and Acquaintances:

- I, too, knew Bishop Pike from my seminary days and feel more like his journey as I left the active church to continue ministry with no committees to restudy the obvious for three years and then restudy it again and again. And still the struggles are present.
- In October 2002, a member of the first group I led to Palestine was, Pike's grandson. On the last day, while in Jaffa, just before we headed to the airport for our flight home, we searched for the tombstone memorial marker of Bishop Pike. No one knew exactly where to go. First we'd been directed to go just above the old town, through a lively schoolyard to an old urban cemetery...no dice. Then we were told to try a cemetery right on the coast, with the sunlit sea crashing behind and below us. The high walls and old rusted metal door, which was locked,

kept us out. Finally we found a guy to open for us. The place was poorly maintained and hard to step around and through the tangle of graves and plants but we had a tip to look near a certain tree. There we found it, Pike's marker, both the sight and the sound of the sea reaching us deep in that walled compound set on a hillside near the shore. Michael got on his knees and brushed off the inscription with his hands. We all prayed and gave thanks. Michael piled a few stones, in Middle Eastern fashion, onto the marker. What a way to end our pilgrimage!

• As I may have mentioned before, Jim Pike served as my father's curate at St. John's, Washington, in the 1940s. He was my first real hero. Here's what I said about him in the autobiography I am writing (in my leisure moments):

There were also other aspects of church life that I found interesting. Not far from St. John's, in nearby Alexandria, Virginia, is one of the Episcopal Church's oldest and most prestigious seminaries. Virginia Theological Seminary (VTS) was established in 1823 and among its founders was Francis Scott Key, whose 1814 poem *The Defense of Fort McHenry*, became the text for the National Anthem of the United States. One of its notable graduates in the 1940s was the Reverend James A. Pike, who became a curate at St. John's following his ordination in 1944. Pike was an unusual ordinand in that he had been divorced and was a convert to Anglicanism from the Roman Catholic Church. He was also a prominent lawyer who had written a standard work on civil law that was in widespread use. In due course he was to become Dean of the Cathedral of St. John the Divine in New York and later, Bishop of California. He was also to become something of a theological pioneer and theologian, so much so that he was accused of heresy! Yet many of the ideas he proposed in his many books seem quite commonplace today, well illustrating the old adage that "Yesterday's heresy becomes today's orthodoxy"

The fact that I had known Jim Pike as a child is a happy irony as it provided me with an early model of what a free-thinking Anglican could be, and I have always been attracted to him, despite some of the perceived foibles of his later years. Although it would be somewhat grandiose to seriously compare myself to him, I can still readily identify with his call for a *demythologized* Church, which was an expression of his view that that traditional Christianity was burdened by what he called *theological baggage*. What was needed, he said, was "not more belief, but fewer beliefs." In my later years I was to embrace similar views, though my own theology was to become far more radical. In a nutshell, I adored this man. I last saw him in New Haven, when he came to preach at Yale.

- Thanks for sharing! With all due respect to Stringfellow and Towne, the *definitive* biography of Jim Pike has not been written. He was, as they say, "a man of many parts." I loved the guy and have hoped to see before I die a complete biography that includes the many extraordinary events in an amazing life of one of our greatest Episcopal leaders.
- Bishop Pike touched my life deeply too. When I was working on the Guaraldi Mass he was very involved and was invaluable in moving an intractable Cathedral along towards actually having this event. I have been reminded of this lately, as one of the opening events of the Monterey Jazz Festival this year is a documentary on Guaraldi, the Mass and me. I have saved many things from the run up to the event, such as correspondence from Pike, Malcolm Boyd and others. Notes from Mark K. Jones,

programs, tickets and lots of photos. The Bishop will be remembered fondly in Monterey.

- I recall my one up-close-and-personal time with Bishop. Pike, I believe on a Saturday evening in the fall of 1960. The rector of St. James Church...asked me to drive Pike from St. James to a motel near a church in Salinas where Jim would officiate the next morning. I was nervous as all get-out with no idea how I could possibly converse with this giant of an intellect for an hour! The good bishop solved my predicament in typical Pikean fashion by doing all the talking, all the smoking, and all the sleeping.... By the time I had moved his suitcase into his motel room, he had opened his briefcase, gotten out some papers, and was already at work on yet another article.

The rector of St. James was dying of cancer. As an Anglo-Catholic, which in those days mostly meant no involvement in social issues, he didn't particularly like Pike. After the rector's death, his widow told me that though their circle of clergy friends disagreed with Pike's stands, it deeply appreciated his pastoral care of the clergy, especially if he knew widows were in financial straits. I wonder how many of Pike's Episcopal and other detractors knew of and honored his deep pastoral sensitivities.

Dear Robert:

That's a touching remembering of James Pike. You wouldn't expect me to agree with all, or much, of it, but I think it belongs in an archive after you polish it up a bit. For instance, to one perusing it the first time it seems there are several voices, or witnesses, speaking. Should there be quote marks in some places, or is it all you? (e.g., Was it your father, or somebody else's father, who was at St. John's, DC?). I think you speak too casually about Pike and the Trinity. That was always a red flag in front of the media (who could no more understand it than the rest of us). The poor bishop need only mention the Trinity than the reporters would say he was denying the doctrine (which, as expressed, we all know isn't so much a *doctrine* as an admission of inability to comprehend the fullness of the Almighty Other). I recall an occasion. c. 1957, when the headlines declared "Pike Denies Trinity" at a sermon at Trinity, NYC (of all places!). A close reading of the article revealed no such thing. Pike was frustrating. Our bishop, in Newark, Leland Stark, thought rightly of himself as an able and engaging, if not original, speaker. He said that at meetings of General Convention or the House of Bishops it might be advertised that Bishop So-and-So would speak at Bygosh Cathedral and would draw perhaps a dozen, whereas Pike could stick a 3"x5" card on an obscure bulletin board saying he would speak in Room 205 and the place would be jammed. Bishops are even more prone to jealousy than the rest of us, and this went against Pike. (But there was a bit of admiration in Leland Stark when he related this). I will not concur that Pike has been vindicated - quite the reverse - and in the end I think his demand to verify himself by attention-seeking will be remembered more than his undoubted gifts. (His career in Poughkeepsie, incidentally, was akin to your woman and the cabin incident, as it turned out). Still, his routing of Vassar's highfalutin president was worth the trip!

Elliott

From my Memoir: I worked for Bishop Pike for three years, from 1963-1966, while he was Bishop of California based in San Francisco. He was one of the most famous and controversial clerics in the United States. In the 1950s Fulton Sheen, Billy Graham and James Pike all had national television programs on religion.

He loved the prominence of being Bishop Pike and the dominance of being a Bishop. He commented on all the important social issues of the fifties and sixties—birth control, abortion, censorship, racism, Israel, Vietnam and sexual freedom. He received a hundred pieces of first-class mail every day, and he insisted all of them be answered. That was one of my jobs. I handled the issues-related letters. I either sent the Bishop's carefully worded public statements or interpreted them to the individual writer. That was intellectually stimulating and made me face my own values and standards as well. I came out of the closet as a screaming liberal, if not a radical.

Pike encouraged me and the other socially conscious clergy to use the media to preach the gospel as it related to social and political concerns.

He was a homophobe for many years and routed out gay clergy from parishes. He later repented, partly due to my influence, and gathered those clergy whom he had persecuted and restored them to ministry.

He had a great sense of humor. When he sponsored a forum on the anniversary of Sigmund Freud's death, someone in the audience reminded the Bishop that Sigmund was an atheist. Pike quipped, "Well, he is not now."

Another time he was preaching at Trinity Church, San Francisco, when he was being tried on heresy charges. An electric spark flashed through the church and the lights went out, and he responded, "I thought they were going to give me a trial first."

He was an alcoholic and a womanizer. Though married, he carried on affairs with women in Toronto, Oakland and several in San Francisco. One woman friend of mine told me that she was summoned to the Bishop's cabin at a conference. He wanted to have sex with her. She gladly submitted saying, "What could I do? I had to obey my Bishop."

He drank heavily, then in the three years before he resigned as Bishop, he attended AA meetings for prominent San Franciscans. He tried marijuana a few times, and in fact I had my first puff with him at a party. He smoked cigarettes feverishly. His huge desk was pock marked with burns. He would light up, get called to the phone, put the butt down and light up another, forgetting where he put the first one. Once I was in a massage class with him. Nude himself massaging his then wife also nude and lying on the table, he insisted on smoking while massaging. I feared the smell of burning flesh.

He had a great intellect and was deeply interested in Christian origins. He traveled often to Israel talking with Jewish and Christian scholars prying into how Christianity got started and how it emerged from Judaism and the Roman Empire. It was on a junket to Israel that he met his death in 1969. He and his wife were in a car that went off the road in the desert. He stayed in a safe place, under some rocks and trees in the shade. While his wife went looking for help, the Bishop must have wandered off and fallen over a cliff to his death.

He was a poor father by his own admission. One of his sons committed suicide. One daughter, frustrated by the Episcopal Church, became a Roman Catholic. Pike and the children's mother, Esther, divorced in 1967.

He loved the liturgy. He expressed his dominance as Bishop by issuing orders about how church services should be run in the Episcopal Church in his Diocese. He introduced the *peace* whereby people in the pews turned and shook hands with the persons nearby. He told the story of the well dressed, gloved and hatted woman in Grace Cathedral. A young man offered to shake her hand, saying, "The peace of the Lord be always with you." She replied, "Oh, not today, thank you."

Bishop Pike challenged traditional beliefs in the church, such as the physical virgin birth and the resurrection of the body of Jesus. He thought the doctrines of the Trinity and Incarnation were outmoded. For this there was an attempt to try him for heresy, but that failed in the House of Bishops. He wrote many books, gave lectures all over the United States and was the darling of the media.

He could be very personal and caring. One time the Bishop borrowed several cigarettes from my wife Lillian saying he would pay her back. Oh yeah, we thought. Sure enough, a few days later a carton of cigarettes came to her by mail from Pike.

Another time, while I was his assistant, he jumped up and said, "Drive me to Palo Alto." He was silent most of the way, and we pulled up to a motel. He was inside about a half hour, got in my car, then we drove back to San Francisco. One of the clergy was drunk, suicidal and holed up in the motel. The busy Bishop was not too busy to call on a sick cleric in need of pastoral care.

Pike was a great influence on my life. He was a fine, troubled, flawed human being. He had a great intellect, sharp wit and deep compassion for people. I miss him still and wish our Bishops today had his moral zeal and public stature.

Don Nakahata

Saturday, March 24, 2012

Dear Alice, Peter, Andrew and John,

I had to leave after the service today as I had another engagement.

I want to add my recollection of Don to the collection you already have.

The last correspondence I had with Don was by email several months ago when he asked permission to use some things I had written in the *Sei Ko Kai* newsletter of which he was editor.

I was saddened to read the article of his death in the *San Francisco Chronicle*.

In 1963, I went to him as my dentist. He had no secretary so he would stop drilling to answer the phone. After he finished working on me he went to the appointment book to make the next time for a visit. Soon he had an office assistant.

One time he gave me a painkiller shot, and I was suddenly cross eyed. He said it would go away, which it did. I think it scared us both. He also worked on the teeth of Lillian and some of my children.

I had learned of his connection to the Episcopal Church in chatting with him in his office. I was shocked when he retired from his practice years later.

One day we had lunch, and he talked with me about what is a healthy mouth? I had raised the question of x-rays. Did we need so many? Are the rays harmful? He said, "You have made me think about what is a healthy mouth." We talked about the ethics of dentistry, and until he retired he used to call me his ethics coach.

Lillian and I were invited to Don and Alice's for dinner one evening in the spring of 1964-5. I had to call and say I might be late as I was planning to be arrested in a sit-in that day at the Cadillac Agency on Van Ness Ave. Five hundred of us were arrested, spent the afternoon in jail then released by dinner time. I was pleased Don was proud of me for doing that. He used to tease me about being late for dinner.

Don spearheaded a drive for congress to grant reparations to Japanese-Americans who had been incarcerated in American Concentration Camps in the United States. I was pleased to get the Vestry of Trinity, San Francisco, to support the resolution before Don got the Bishop's Committee of *Se Ko Kai* to do so.

I had heard from Christmas letters or through the grapevine that Don had heart problems. We got regular

Christmas-card photos of Alice and Don and sometimes of the boys on a mountaintop somewhere.

I felt privileged to be at the service today and hear so much more about Donald as a mentor, teacher, father, father figure, husband and family man.

I wish I had known him better and kept up a closer relationship. I am proud to have known him and sad that he has died.

He, like Pastor David Hawbecker, the preacher, and I question the whole religious thing yet are firm in a commitment to a long tradition of believers who use our minds, brains and intellect and enjoy the search and questioning of creation, life, love, forgiveness and life after death. I like the Book of Common Prayer's deliciously ambiguous statement. I have a "sure and certain hope" of life after death.

Warmest regards and sympathies,

Some Recollections about Eugen Stech

Wednesday, January 21, 2009

Eugen Stech, an ordained priest of the Episcopal Church, canonically resident in the Diocese of California, a long time resident of Berkeley, California, died on January 16, 2009, at Summit Hospital in Oakland, CA. He was about eighty-three-years old. He was ill for many years with lung and breathing problems. After he left the employ of the church in the early '70s, he was employed in the Church Divinity School of the Pacific and the Graduate Theological Union bookstore.

Monday, November 27, 2006. I wrote the following in my journal.
Eugen Stech – Man of Mystery

I have known Stech since the late sixties when he was vicar of St. Barnabas and I was at St. Aidan's. He was married then with two sons from his wife's previous marriage. I didn't know him very well even though he lived right down the street from us on Amber Drive. Because he was a graduate of Nashotah House and quite Anglo-Catholic in outlook, I, as a broad church liberal, felt little in common with him. I even thought he didn't like me very much, and I can't say I was very fond of him. We had little connection.

One of his stepsons accompanied my former wife, Lillian, and my children when they left me and San Francisco driving in the VW bus for the east coast after our divorce in 1969. My children were fond of the boy, but I believe they have lost all track of him. Gene apparently divorced and left St. Barnabas about the same time I left the active ministry.

I resigned from St. Aidan's in 1970, and went into private practice as a marriage and family therapist until 1983. I lost track of Gene in the early seventies. I ran across him a few times seeing him at work at the bookstore of the Graduate Theological Union in Berkeley. He seemed to avoid looking at me or talking with me.

A couple of years ago we got in contact and exchanged phone calls and later emails. I found him difficult to talk with. He evaded questions, interrupted me when I was talking and was rather negative about church and politics. He also seemed somewhat paranoid about what might happen to him. We had lunch together once, breakfast once and coffee another time. I visited his small apartment twice in Berkeley where he lives in housing designed for Lutheran seminary students. Rather ironic given his Anglo Catholic heritage.

I call him a man of mystery, because I could never get much out of him about his life and thoughts. He was very reluctant to tell me his age. He told me once; I forgot and, when I asked him again, he hesitated. I never knew much about his marriage, his divorce, his personal life after marriage, his finances and even his health. I must ask him why he avoided me when he saw me at the bookstore. Until recently I knew nothing of his life as a young man, his parents or friends.

I know this is my problem as I am very curious about the personal details of people's lives. Part of being a therapist and a pastor is dealing with people with problems. Also I had the experience at Esalen in 1969, where we practiced open and honesty in our daily lives. I expect people to be that way with me even thought we have no agreement to be that way with each other.

As time has gone by, I have become very fond of Stech and slowly have learned a lot about him. He told me about a woman friend in Berkeley with whom he had a good relationship for a while and then something happened and they no longer see each other.

He has told me about his grandfather and father who were ministers in the Lutheran and Calvinist tradition in the Evangelical and Reformed Church in the Midwest.

He apparently had some valuable Escher paintings, which he sold and feels he was cheated. He has some friends in Czechoslovakia whom he has visited and feels close to now.

He has told me about his lung problems, which cause him to be weak and depressed sometimes. He is worried that he is dependent on his neighbors to get him food, to go shopping and do chores with him.

He admires my frankness in *Sex Priest* but has told me little of the behaviors, joys and sadness of his sex and personal life.

Because of his breathing problems he has not ventured far from Berkeley and has not been to San Francisco for years.

Friday, June 27, 2008

Trying to get some clergy friends to visit Gene I wrote the following:

Eugen Stech

I call him Gene. Perhaps you should ask him what he would like to be called. He is rather reserved and cautious in relating to people. He is not very self-revealing. He is perhaps just shy. I have known him since 1965, but with long lapses of not seeing or hearing from him.

He graduated from Nashotah House Episcopal Seminary and is an ordained priest of the Episcopal Church. He served the now-defunct St. Barnabas Church in the Excelsior District of San Francisco. He left the active ministry in about 1970 and worked for many years in the Graduate Theological Union Bookstore.

He retired a number of years ago and has lived in an apartment in Berkeley. He seems to have few friends. He and I hooked up again by email and have corresponded regularly for the last eight years. I have visited him several times in Berkeley. He has refused to come to San Francisco to meet me. He says he cannot travel because of ill health.

He has severe lung problems that keep him weak and tired a lot of the time. He is presently housebound in a small retirement facility in El Cerrito. He has a woman friend who helped him move when he could no longer maintain himself in his apartment.

He is mentally quick and alert with a great interest in politics and current events. He uses his computer for being in touch with me and perhaps others.

He is thin, about 5'10" tall, with thinning gray hair. He has a ready smile when he is relaxed. He has a good sense of humor when he allows it to show. He has a thin craggy face and good teeth—I think.

While he is sick and lonely, he has enough sense to acknowledge regularly that he is thankful for what he has when he sees and hears of people who are so much worse off than he is.

I have stayed in contact with him but have tried to keep him as responsible for himself as possible. When he was having trouble in his last apartment, I suggested he get in contact with Berkeley Social Services, but I do not know if he ever did.

Some Ideas on How to Approach Him
The first approach should be by email.

Ask him how he would like to be addressed. Do not ask him where he lives or for his phone number until you sense he would like to talk further.

Tell him who you are and how you were referred to him. Tell him that you know me or that you have heard of me. He trusts me and has asked me to find someone in the East Bay to have contact with him—by email.

I believe he wants some more human contact. He has told me he is lonely. The facility where he is staying has only two other "guests." I also know he has few friends or acquaintances.

Ask him to tell you about himself. The less information you use that I have related to you the better. He may get cranky if he thinks I have revealed more of his background than he might wish.

He is a good, humorous gentleman who has been crippled in some way by secrecy and perhaps by paranoia and fear of revealing himself to others.

Good luck and many thanks. Please let me know if I can be of any help to you or to Gene.

Here is an email I saved from our correspondence. Swing was the Episcopal Bishop in the Diocese of California, where Gene was canonically resident but inactive. Let him speak for himself.

Subject: PLEASE RAISE SWINGS CONSCIOUSNESS

Date: Sun, 29 Nov 1998 02:56:13 -0800

From: Max Stech
To: CROMEY

Roberto,

I have just scanned the last Bps news letter ....Jaysus I'm

sure the White House is really disturbed when they read that
Swing wants Clinton to resign.

*You have more clout with Swing than I ever will. Ask
him where he was when that ass-hole G. Bush was bombing
Panama? Did he suggest that Bush resign.??????????????*

*Killing all those Panamanians was far worse than getting
a blow job in the Oval Office toilet or wherever that deed
occurred.*

Whats with these Republicans anyway.?????????????????

Reagan and Bush lied frequently about matters of import.

EAS

PS Why do I read these church publications??????????????

Rest in peace old friend Stech.

Paul Moore—My Hero

A dozen of us were in the Park Avenue apartment of Paul and
Jenny Moore the summer of 1951. The place was bare, no chairs
rugs or lamps. I was disappointed, as I was impressed to be
invited to a Park Avenue apartment. I had heard Moore was
rich. Those present were all the summer staff of the Lower East
Side Mission of Trinity, Wall Street and Grace Church, Jersey
City, where Moore lead a team ministry ministering to a poor
and distressed neighborhood. We were gathered for a party,
pizza, beer and sodas arrived, and we picnicked on the floor.
C. Kilmer Myers and other clergy were also present along with
the Moores.

I had read of Moore's ministry; coming from great wealth,
he chose to live with his large family in an open rectory in
that tough neighborhood. I was raised in poor neighborhoods
in Brooklyn and Queens. My father was an underpaid priest
of the Diocese of Long Island, but we loved the city. Articles
in the *Living Church, the Episcopalian* and the *New York Times*

glamorized urban work in the cities as the frontier ministry in those days.

I was a student at New York University, Washington Square; Moore, Myers and Pike came to the Canterbury Club and spoke to student gatherings. I was inspired by their stories about the poor, gangs, blacks and narcotic addicts. They helped me see the relationship between the gospel of Jesus and the social situation we lived in.

Paul led a quiet Day at General Theological Seminary sometime during my first or second year. I dozed through boring meditations and periods of quiet. I came alive when he told stories of ministry to human beings in the city. I heard him preach here and there in the city over the years.

I lost track of him when he went to Indianapolis to be dean there. I was delighted when he was elected Suffragan of Washington D.C. In 1967 I was a fellow of the College of Preachers in D.C. for six weeks. He invited me to dinner at his home with Jenny and all nine of his children. It was fun to be there, and I was honored to be invited.

My father was a chaplain on Welfare Island, and Paul asked him to take one of his old teachers from St. Paul's School under his wing. His name was Fred Bartrop. He had been thrown out of St. Paul's, because he was gay and an alcoholic. Paul paid for Barstow's rent and food for a while and had him work with my father in the hospitals on Welfare Island.

I knew Paul had been involved with an organization to help homosexuals. I was impressed by his daring and willingness to work with the untouchables.

I was thrilled when he was elected to the Bishop of New York. In 1978 I wrote and asked him if there were any jobs I could apply for in the Diocese of New York. I was ready to leave San Francisco and come back to New York where I belonged. He said there were none. I was disappointed but am happy how it all worked out for me anyway.

We kept in touch by mail. He supported me when I challenged the church and Bishop Swing on gay rights and marriage issues. He said he thought Swing was way off base in his opposition to what I was doing, but he asked me not to reveal that to anyone. I didn't.

A couple of his children lived in the San Francisco Bay Area, and he visited out here from time to time. He preached at Grace Cathedral. I invited him several times to preach at Trinity, San Francisco, but he always turned me down. I was disappointed but went on doing what I do and did.

We tried to connect for a drink or lunch a few times when I visited NewYork, but it never worked out. I knew he liked and respected me and my work and vision. We were of a different social class, and he preferred his own as they say. I always loved and respected him and still do. When Honor Moore, his daughter, outed him, I felt sad that so much of his life was closeted and his deception hurt his family. He is still my hero and had a great impact on my life and ministry. For that and him I remain truly grateful.

Here is a letter I wrote to Honor Moore, which she never answered. I see there are a few details in it that I have already mentioned.

Wednesday, February 27, 2008

Dear Honor Moore,

> I think your outing of Paul Moore is just wonderful. He has always been one my heroes and now even more so. I am sad he lived so much of his life in the closet. I wish he had announced the gay part of himself to the world. What a comfort it would have been to gays and lesbians and an inspiration to the closeted to come out.
>
> C. Kilmer Myers with whom Paul worked in the '50s, and who later became Bishop of California, tried marriage, adopted children and was also gay. My bet is that his alcoholism was his attempt to cover up this gay side. I have second-hand testimony that Myers acted out sexually as a gay man while he was Bishop. He, too, is

one of my heroes for his passionate concern for the poor, homeless and victims of injustice.

My own father, the Reverend E. Warren Cromey was bi-sexual. He adored my mother and loved my brother and me but had gay sex from time to time with friends who later told me about those activities.

My father was chaplain on Welfare Island (now Roosevelt Island) in the '50s and '60s. Paul Moor referred his old St. Paul's teacher, Fred Batrop, to my dad for counseling and friendship. I remember meeting Fred once or twice at our house for dinner. I do believe Fred was alcoholic and gay but had not married. I also recollect Fred was a priest deposed for some reason I have forgotten.

I also know that Paul was on the board of directors of a counseling center to help homosexual men and women in the '50s. It was based for a long time at the now defunct Church of the Holy Communion in Chelsea. When I discovered this, I thought how brave Paul was to ally himself so early with a homosexual organization.

I had no personal knowledge or suspicions about Paul's homosexual side. His pro-gay stands and actions as bishop were just another natural part of his concern for the poor and disenfranchised.

Paul came to General Theological Seminary a couple of times between 1953-56 when I was a student there. He led a quiet day and tried to teach us to meditate. He failed miserably as far I was concerned. Whenever I am forced to meditate I fall asleep or think of sex. But when he came and talked about the ministry of the church to the inner city and urban concerns, I was excited and inspired to spend my ministry in the city. I have served in the Bronx and then in the city of San Francisco since 1962.

Your article about Paul's life re-inspired and reminded me about the work for justice, peace and care for the poor all over again. I am married, straight and have had a long ministry with gay and lesbians here in San Francisco since 1964 as a matter of fact. My San Francisco parish was seventy-five percent gay men and five percent lesbian and a few of us straight people as well.

Beth Clements told me a couple of years ago that you were working on a book about your father. I do hope the *New Yorker* article does move toward a book.

Thank you for writing the article. In many ways it continues the importance of Paul's life and ministry

With all good wishes,

Robert

Ruth Brinker, R.I.P.

Ruth Brinker used the Trinity kitchens in the early 1980s cooking for Meals on Wheels. Her hair was always perfect—silver gray. Her dresses were always tasteful and colorful. Occasionally she wore an apron but always over a dress. She was cheerful and smart. In 1983, she met me in the hallway outside of the Collier Room and told me she delivered ten meals to ten of her acquaintances who had AIDS and were so weak they could not prepare food for themselves. A week later she said she had prepared and delivered twenty meals. She asked me if she could continue to cook at Trinity and have the meals sent out. I said sure.

Meals were soon sent out every day, and she had a squad of volunteers to deliver the meals. Each week more and more meals went out to feed men who had AIDS. Restaurants donated food; the Food Bank and other sources provided food. She raised money and her purse was her bank. She went on radio and television in San Francisco, Los Angeles and New York.

Newspapers carried the story. She called her program Project Open Hand. It grew too large to be housed at Trinity, and about four years later it moved into its own facilities. A board of directors was established, and a new director took over a decade after Ruth Brinker funded Project Open Hand. Ruth died on August 8, 2011.

A Recollection in Memory of the Reverend Michael Smith, Licensed Practical Nurse

Michael Smith says he met me when I arrived in my VW to perform a wedding at Holy Innocent, San Francisco, where the scheduled cleric was a no-show. I don't remember that but do recollect Nina and him coming to dinner at 56 Amber Drive when I was vicar of St. Aidan's, San Francisco.

Michael was born in England; his father was in the British Army. He and his wife lived in India many years before Michael's birth. He went to college and studied theology in England.

He told us that he and Nina wanted to marry in England. As a seminarian, he could not expect to get ordained if his fiancé was divorced, which Nina was. He came to California, and Bishop Pike ordained him in the early 1960s.

He became curate at Christ Church, Alameda, where he ran the youth group. He invited me to come and speak to the group on urban ministry and civil rights. His boss, Wolfe Hodgkin, chastised him for inviting Cromey, that radical, to talk to the youth. Michael and Wolfe did not get along, and Michael soon moved on to work construction. He was disillusioned by the church's treatment of him and Nina. Wolfe's son became a good friend and smoking buddy over the years.

Nina and Michael then made jewelry and followed the street fairs all over California. I would run into them from time to time selling their wares in front of Ghiradelli Square. Tiring of the fairs, Michael decided to become a Licensed Vocational Nurse. Nina was not happy with that decision, and for a number of reasons they broke up. Michael gave Nina their house, a Victorian on Duncan Street.

Michael immediately loved being a hands-on nurse working with mentally and emotionally disturbed teens.

A crack table-tennis player, Michael challenged by the kids, would proceed to beat them royally at the game. He with the other nurses from time to time had to physically restrain the kids when they became violent and threatening.

The story of Audrey and Michael's meeting and courtship is the stuff of a fairy tale. Michael loved Golden Gate Park. One sunny day he went into the Japanese Tea Garden enjoying its red and yellow leaves, the arch bridge and the green-and-yellow, straw-thatched teahouse. Audrey Wood was sipping her tea. Michael took his and they began a conversation that went something like this.

Michael. What are you doing these days?

Audrey. I'm a student at the Church Divinity School in Berkeley.

Michael. Are you planning too be a priest?

Audrey. Yes, I hope to be ordained in the Episcopal Church.

Michael. I am a priest of the Episcopal Church.

Audrey. Really?

Michael. Yes, but I work at St. Mary's Hospital as a nurse now.

So the conversation continued, and the relationship flourished. When they married, Michael Smith and Audrey Woods became Michael and Audrey Woodsmith.

When Audrey came to Trinity as a seminarian, Michael decided to give the church another chance. After attending for a while, he began to take the 8:00 AM service.

He told me one day, "Robert, if I say I will do something, you can depend on me to do and be on time." He continued, "I'll also tell you this, I will always be loyal to you, I'll never criticize you behind your back" To my knowledge he kept those promises.

Michael and I used to have dinner or lunch together every month. We both loved Indian food, and we'd eat at the Nan 'n Curry on Irving Street. He had decided opinions on a number of things.

He'd say, "Robert, see this coat, I got it at Good Will. It is a $500 coat and I got for $75.00." He loved a bargain.

He would scowl and proclaim, "Robert, no gentleman puts ice cubes in single malt scotch." Putting some cubes into my Glenlivet, I said, "I do." He'd look properly offended.

The Cromeys and the Woodsmiths often dined together. Audrey finished seminary and did not get ordained. Both Michael and Audrey were terribly upset. Audrey went on to become a high-school English teacher gaining tenure at Fremont High School. They bought a home there, and Michael commuted to St. Mary's until he was felled by illness.

Michael had a tough exterior and often a gruff manner. I attributed some of it to his having a British Army career sergeant for a father. Below the surface he was kind, gentle and caring. While at Trinity several couples sought him out to perform their marriage ceremony. When I was very sick in 2004, he came to visit me almost every day. He also visited Michael Patterson from Trinity and Aidan Hansen from Ann's school when they were patients at St. Mary's. They are only the ones I know about. I always felt he loved, supported and cared for Ann and me. I trusted him completely.

In 2004 I was quite sick. After abdominal surgery, I had a psychotic episode for a week. One of the days Michael came to see me I was refusing to get out of bed and into a chair. Michael said, "Robert, do as you are told." I snarled back. "Do you who I am? Don't you dare talk to me like that." Michael smiled knowingly.

He supported Audrey as she finished seminary and went on for a Master's Degree in English, then worked in a couple of schools before landing in Fremont. He idolized her and showed it with his steady glance and attention to her. She also adored him. The twenty-eight-year difference in their ages seemed to make no difference. I loved it that as a Brit he disdained France. When he and Audrey went to Paris a few years ago, he confessed to absolutely loving that city—even more than London.

For a time Michael lived in their apartment on Third Avenue four nights a week and went home to Fremont for the weekends. He grew to hate the time alone and away from Audrey. He and I often had dinner one evening a week. He was not comfortable at Trinity under the new interim and stopped attending. He told me that he had tried renewing his connection to the church at Trinity; now he was giving it up."

He often talked of his love for his theological college in England and the emphasis on ministry to the sick and poor. He had a rigorous training to be a priest at the school. He reminded me that he had experience at the Urban Training Center in Chicago. He had done work with youth gangs and had marched in Selma, Alabama, in 1964. Now he felt he was best at being a nurse at this juncture in his life.

He and Audrey went to Paris again this summer of 2011. He got sick, spent time in the hospital there and returned home. He soon was too sick to work at St. Mary's. He spent several weeks at home breathing with the help of oxygen. Audrey's mother, Jody Woods, spent almost every day with Michael for three months so that Audrey could continue to work and he would not be left alone. Even before that they had a good relationship and he would never hear a negative word said about mothers-in-law. Soon Michael had to be hospitalized; he died Sunday November 20, 2011, in the hospital in Fremont, California. His wife Audrey was present. He was 70.

ISRAEL

Israel and Jews

I suppose everyone brought up in the United States is an anti-Semite, including some Jews. The anti-Semitism of Europe was exported to the United States with all the immigrants from Europe and Russia. Discrimination against Jews in schools, colleges and graduate schools was relentless. There are still lots of gentile-only country clubs and beachfronts. There are also now Jewish-only social clubs.

I was introduced to anti-Jewish sentiment with some vehemence when I attended St. Paul's School. We athletes were urged to beat the "Jew Bastards," "Yids," "Kikes" or whatever other epithets we hurled against our opponents from New-York-area prep schools. I was embarrassed by the remarks but didn't stand up for my Jewish brothers and sisters.

At Colgate University where I spent an unhappy semester 1949-50. Bob Shostack was one of my roommates. A Jew from Newburgh, New York, Bob was not rushed by any of the fraternities. Gentile, I received six invitations from fraternities. By then I had transferred from Colgate to New York University in Greenwich Village. The school was called "NY Jew" by everyone, Jews and all. The school was eighty-five percent Jewish, ten percent Roman Catholic and five percent everyone else. Half the swim team, where I ended up as captain, was Jewish.

I have vivid memories of the newsreels of the concentration camps in Germany and Poland. The bodies of thousand upon thousands of Jews and others piled high were appalling. The tangled piles of eyeglasses photographed spoke of the sheer numbers of the dead. Stories of discrimination at home and abroad shocked me. We had a few Jewish friends. My mother's best friend was Jewish—Sylvia, who was the widow of Italian Bill Palmagiano.

I supported the new nation of Israel and was lacking in understanding of the rage of the displaced Palestinians.

I spoke and wrote against anti-Jewish sentiments in our church and country all during my ministry. I am glad most of the institutions of American society are open to Jews. It was a long time coming and still needs guarding.

I am in trouble with some of my Jewish friends, because I am very critical of the Israel's treatment of the Palestinians. Many Jews in the United States and in Israel are also distressed with the policies of the Israeli government.

The intransigence of many Palestinians and Israelis has created an almost impossibly hostile climate resulting in maiming, death and destruction in both lands.

After some horrific Israeli attacks on Palestinians, I wrote a letter published in the *San Francisco Chronicle* saying I have climbed down off the fence and declared myself a Palestinian. I had heard the stories of a Palestinian Roman Catholic priest and a Palestinian Anglican priest. Both tell the story of being told to leave their homes on very short notice and to take their belongings, then watched their homes bulldozed to make way for Israeli settlers.

This situation today is another war of the rich and the poor. The Israelis are rich with a three-billion-dollar subsidy from the U.S. government. The Palestinians are among the poorest people on earth.

I have no illusion that the Palestinian leadership is open to compromise and discussion any more than conservative

Israelis are. However, I must take a stand on one side or the other and make my protest known. It is another way of keeping the pressure on decision makers to make sense and make peace happen. To be in the middle is the place of silence and the yielding to oppression.

"I am a Palestinian"

With Israel's Prime Minister Netanyahu's visit to the United States I have received a number of emails from friends in support of Israel. I replied to one with the following email reiterating my long held and unwavering position. Years ago I said, "I am a Palestinian."

> Let's not forget we have agreed not to haunt each other with propaganda. I think the Israeli government's treatment of the Palestinians has been horrific. Camps, military brutality, breaking agreements, walls, building on disputed property, constant hindering negotiations and disregarding United Nation's mandates all hinder peace and tranquility in Israel. The U.S. Congress pandering to Netanyahu was ludicrous. I hope President Mahmoud Abbas of the Palestinian Authority will also be invited to address a joint session of Congress.

> Israel's leaders have refused to negotiate with the Palestinians until they repudiate Hamas, a group democratically elected to leadership by the people. In addition Israeli leaders have indicated they would not negotiate with any group who does not believe in the right of Israel to exist.

> Negotiating about those two important issues should be exactly what the discussions should be about. People of good will can sit down and deal with the hardest issues. There must not be preconditions to talking together. The refusal to do so smacks of not wanting to negotiate under any circumstances.

Lest you think I am just one more anti-Israeli-government crank, please note these web sites of Jews and others who support Palestinians.

- http://jfjfp.com/ (Jews for Justice for Palestinians)
- http://www.tikkun.org (Rabbi Michael Lerner)
- http://www.womeninblack.org/en/about (Women in Black: For Justice. Against the War.)
- http://jewishvoiceforpeace.org (Jewish Voice for Peace)

Israel Invaded by Arab Countries

If Arab countries or Iran invaded Israel, what would the U.S. government do? We would honor our long time commitment to aid Israel. That seems like a simple answer. The recent wild reception of the Prime Minister of Israel by the U.S. Congress leads us to be assured that such support would be forthcoming.

However, after the disaster of a ten-year debacle in Iraq and Afghanistan, would the America people really support sending our troops and spending billions of dollars to yet another war in the Middle East?

Pressure on the President and the Congress by wealthy Jewish supporters of Israel would be tremendous. Elected officials would fear that any opposition to sending U.S. soldiers back into the Middle East would cost their reelection. Politics and money would top reason and restraint in responding to such a threat to Israel. Leaving it to the United Nations would not be seen as real support.

Most Jews and I still sense a strong anti-Semitic streak running through Middle America.

In June 2002, a nationwide survey released by the Anti-Defamation League (ADL) resulted in the following. The findings in brief—Strongly anti-Semitic:

17% of Americans

35% of Hispanics

35% of African-Americans

3% of U.S. college and university students

The 2005 Survey of American Attitudes Towards Jews in America, a national poll of 1,600 American adults conducted in March 2005, found that 14% of Americans - or nearly 35 million adults - hold views about Jews that are 'unquestionably anti-Semitic,' compared to 17% in 2002, Previous ADL surveys over the last decade had indicated that anti-Semitism was in decline. In 1998, the number of Americans with hardcore anti-Semitic beliefs had dropped to 12% from 20 % in 1992.[5]

For 2007, FBI figures show that among 1,477 religiously motivated hate crimes reported by U.S. law enforcement authorities, 9% were anti-Islamic, 9.5% were anti-other religion, 4.4% were anti-Catholic and, by far outstripping any other category, 68.4% were anti-Jewish.[6]

Some people decry a new anti-Semitism. They are liberals who are opposed to the Israeli government's policies toward the Palestinians or who call for a boycott of Israeli products as a fight against these policies. This group would oppose another war.

As an antiwar activist, I would oppose such a new war. But more important, I suspect a war to support Israel in the near future would not gain popular support. But there is time to negotiate.

A willingness to negotiate and deal with the concrete issues is certainly needed to show the people of the Unites States and the rest of the world that Israel is serious about ending discrimination against the Palestinians and seeking peace. Such action would put off any nation's desire to invade Israel and assure protection if Israel was invaded.

Jewish Friends and Israel

I have a number of Jewish friends. They are committed to Israel's existence and support. Some are of the opinion that Israel can do no wrong; some are critical of Israeli policies

5 http://en.wikipedia.org/wiki/Antisemitism_in_the_United_States
6 (Forbes Magazine 1/22/09)

toward the Palestinians and some say that because I am not a Jew, I just *don't understand.* A couple of Jewish friends have joined me in saying, "Well let's just be friends and not talk about the subject." One has said he does not want this divisive issue to stand in the way of our friendship. Yet from time to time some Jewish friends send me an item about Israel they cannot resist sharing. I have done the same.

I have devised a new strategy for myself. I will write my ideas and thoughts about Israel and the Palestinians on my blog. I will not notify Jews I care about when I add items. If they want to know what I think they can look at my blog from time to time to find out.

From time to time I write letters to the editor expressing my opinion about Israel. Sometimes they are printed.

I expect no amount of argument or discussion will change anyone's mind or opinion about the Palestinians and the Israeli government's policies. For Jews, Israel is a deeply emotional issue tied to memories, history, traditions and ethnic origins. Many Jewish and Gentile scholars and writers have testified to this phenomenon. Passion transcends reason, especially about Israel. As one Jewish friend, a physician and scientist, wrote, "My balls are in Israel."

My response is "My balls are with the Palestinians." I hope I will always stand with the poor and oppressed wherever they are. Israel is not oppressed as it has the strongest military in the region and up until now the total allegiance of the United State government.

I decry the fact that there is a great silence among many politicians and indeed friends of mine about the extent of the U.S. support of Israel. There is a fear of being dubbed an anti-Semite. There is a growing notion among some Jews that criticism of Israel is just a new form of anti-Semitism. I will let my Jewish friends decide if that is the way they would describe me. In any case I will not be silent about my views.

So in the hope of preserving friendship, my opinions on the Israeli—Palestinian issue will appear on my blog and perhaps in a letter to the editor, but I will refrain from sending them to friends directly.

Forbidden Topic

Politicians seldom criticize Israel. They don't want to offend Jews who have power and money. The belief is that Jews will be against attempts to give less money to Israel. Offending Jews is political suicide. We saw Hilary Rodham Clinton disagree publicly with the White House when the US government was critical of Israel. It was said she was afraid of offending Jews in New York State where she was running for the senate.

I wonder if it is true that Jews vote as a block? It seems like conventional political wisdom not to offend Jews or any other minority. Certainly an anti-gay candidate could not win office in San Francisco. Yes there are rich and powerful lesbians and gays, but there are thousands of straight people who support homosexual rights. An anti-Semite also would not get elected in San Francisco or any other major American city. Gentiles would join Jews by the score to defeat such a candidate.

The notion that Jews vote in blocks is another form of anti-Semitism. Jews are not seen as individual, human beings. They are seen as a race, an ethnic group or a religion and are the target of hate groups. Ugly epithets are hurled at Jews by the sick, the evil and the know-nothings. "Jews band together and take care of their own. Money hungry, Christ killers, sharp at business, pushy and aggressive" are expressions all too familiar to anti-Semites and their Jewish victims.

In my experience I see that Jews are Democrats and Republicans, conservative, liberal, hard working and lazy. Jews are noted for having a wide variety of opinions on many subjects. A popular Jewish saying is wherever there are ten Jews arguing, you get twenty different opinions. Jews are witty and boorish, charming and klutzy, beautiful and homely, make good doctors and bad ones, sexy and cold, rich and poor—just like the rest of the human beings on the planet.

No doubt most Jews support the nation of Israel and want to see it flourish, but many Jews in the United States and Israel are appalled by the tactics of the Israeli government and military. The exclusive policies of some Israeli Conservative Jews are quite unpopular among liberal and non- religious Jews here and abroad.

Criticizing Israel and talk of withholding or reducing of U.S. tax dollars to Israel are forbidden topics of conversation for our politicians. I suggest this is another form of anti-Semitism and treating Jews in a less than human way.

Israel's policies of keeping Palestinians as second class citizens, maintaining huge refugee camps, systematic taking over of Palestinian citizen's property, the killing of Palestinian civilians by the military, overtly assassinating suspected terrorists—all the while taking billions of U.S. tax-payers dollars—are facts of life that many Americans and Israelis dislike immensely. Jews, Christians, Muslims and secularists in the United States and Israel oppose these outrages against humanity, but our politicians, afraid of the so-called Jewish vote, regard the topic as forbidden. That attitude in itself is anti-Semitic.

We need an open discussion of the relations between the United States and Israel. Foreign-policy experts and politicians need to hear the concerns of American Jews, Christians, Muslims and secularists who want to support Israel but are more and more negative about the current relations between the Israeli government and the Palestinians

Jews Control the Media

As a frequent critic of Israeli tactics against Palestinians, I have had a number of letters to the editor and short articles printed in various newspapers. Certainly not all that I have written has been published. I get occasional letters and phone calls from Muslims and Christians supporting my position. I also get a few letters and phone calls from Jews who criticize my stances. I assume they are Jews by their surname. I could be wrong, of course.

My supporters say that the plight of Palestinians is not covered well in the local news. The bravery of the Israelis is emphasized. Palestinians are depicted as terrorists while Israelis are defenders of freedom or some such. They go on to say this is because the Jews control the media.

It may be that many media-leaders are Jewish. I do not pretend to have accurate statistics about such matters. Assuming for a moment that media moguls are Jewish, so what!

The assumption that Jews control the media is that there is a Jewish conspiracy to slant the news in favor of Israel. Behind that is the idea that Jews would all agree on a program completely supporting Israel.

I have read in the American media about sharp critics of Israeli policies by Israeli Jewish citizens. There is a strong Jewish protest movement in Israel to find peace and reconciliation with Palestinians. The peace and justice movement is also voluble in that country.

This past Chanukah, my wife and I were at a dinner party at the home of Jewish friends. There were eight for dinner and three of us were Gentiles. A rather fierce discussion erupted among the Jews present about the value of Chanukah. All said they thought it should be a home celebration and not something presented in Union Square or other public places. Yet we know there are many other Jews who love the public display. Jews vary widely in their attitudes about everything, including Israel.

Rabbi Michael Lerner's *Tikkum* magazine and his books reflect strong American Jewish support for Israel but are sharply critical of Israeli policies and tactics toward Palestinians. Other American groups are critical of the Israeli government's actions.

If Jewish moguls are in charge of television and movies, they should be ashamed of themselves. It is not that they are pro-Israel but that they wallow in garbage. The pap and violence that dominates those media are a discredit to the sensibilities and intellect of the American people. My Jewish friends are just as appalled by the misuse of those media as I am. The cultural and intellectual character of Jews in this country runs contrary to every aspect of modern radio, television and motion pictures.

I do not see a conspiracy on the part of Jews in the media to be pro-Israel. Jews vary widely in their opinions about everything just like all thoughtful and intelligent people do. I doubt if Bill Clinton gathered all the Jews who are major players in the mass media, he could get them to agree on a common policy on Israel.

Most Jews probably want Israel to continue to exist. But many Jews are not happy with present Israeli policies. That is true also among Jews in the media.

Holocaust Industry

The story of the concentration camps in Germany, Poland and Russia and the killing of millions of Jews, homosexuals, mentally disabled and political prisoners must be told and retold in each generation. This must never again happen. Sadly, we know such mass killings continue in many places in the world.

There has grown up in the United States and perhaps elsewhere what has been called *a holocaust industry*. Its purpose is to tell and retell the story so no one will ever forget what happened in Germany in the 1940s. The Nazis led the way in attempting to exterminate the Jews and others they deemed their enemies. However, hardly a week goes by when there is not a new book or movie or television show that depicts the horrors of the camps.

My criticism of the holocaust industry is that I feel saturated with this information. Education is one thing; saturation is another. I feel overwhelmed with the sheer production of the information.

I resent that the industry has tried to usurp the word, *holocaust*, and have it only apply to what happened to Jews in the 1940s. *Holocaust* is a word that has to do with destruction by fire. It has taken on the meaning of the mass destruction by any means of Jews. There was a holocaust of nine million Native

Americans over three hundred years in the United States. Southeast Asia and Africa have seen the mass destruction of people. They are also *holocausts.*

The holocaust industry has severely played down the killing of Protestant and Catholic clergy, homosexuals and the physically and mentally disabled in the concentration camps and gas ovens. We must never forget the other millions murdered by the Nazis.

My final gripe is that the word, *anti-Semite,* now refers only to Jews. I want to point out that all the Arabs are Semites. There are those who have tried to co-opt that word, *Semite,* too.

Now there are Jews who have the same gripes. But it is hard for them to admit it. They have relatives who perished in the camps. They know the pain and sorrow more directly than I do. But there it is. I get to express my annoyance with those who try to usurp words and historical events as belonging only to Jews.

Holocaust Overkill

A holocaust survivor, Roman Rakover, awaits a U.S. Supreme Court decision in a complicated case that may award him money from an insurance policy paid for by his father who died in a Siberian Camp in the 1940s. This certainly is a righteous cause, and I hope he wins the case.

This is an important holocaust story. However, I find the endless media attention to the holocaust counterproductive. Hardly a week goes by without another story, book, movie, video, novel, poem, painting, sculpture, dance or other depiction of some aspect of the *Holocaust.*

Certainly, we should never forget the horrific extermination of six million Jews by the Nazi regime. Certainly, we must continue to educate the old and young about those terrible events perpetrated by the enormously well educated and cultured German society. Certainly, we must root out and expose every kind of anti-Semitism. We cannot condone those who say the holocaust never happened.

I lived in Germany for a year in the 1970s. I heard good German people in denial, saying they never heard of the extermination while it was going on. Mr. Born was in the German Army and lost a lung on the Russian front. He said he never heard of the camps until after the war.

On three occasions I visited *Dachau*, the concentration camp just out side of Munich. It is like going the distance to Daly City from San Francisco. There is even a trolley that is marked *Dachau* in big letters. I took my teenage daughters to expose them to the horrors memorialized there. I visited the holocaust memorial, *Yad Vashem*, in Jerusalem. I have read extensively in the history of Germany and the Nazis.

From my youth, the anti-Semitism of my prep school and college pals in the 1940s and '50s horrified me. In my work as a priest of the Episcopal Church, I have written and spoken against the wretched anti-Semitism in our American church and society. I'll even use the dreaded cliché: Some of my best friends are Jews. My Internist, Ophthalmologist, Otolaryngologist, (ear, nose and throat specialist), Podiatrist, Orthopedic Surgeon, Real Estate Broker, Stock Broker and Lawyer are Jewish.

Philip Roth in one of his novels uses the expression *holocaust industry* to describe groups who perpetuate the horrible memories. The industry has tried to usurp the word, *holocaust.* The dictionary defines it as a sacrifice consumed by fire, a thorough destruction by fire. Most victims were gassed or shot, then their bodies were often burned but also buried in the ground.

When the destruction of the Federal Building in Oklahoma City, September 1, 2000, was referred to as a holocaust, there were objections. When Native Americans and Armenians use the word *holocaust* about their experiences, some people in the industry object, indicating holocaust is reserved alone for the massacre of Jews in Europe.

The industry seems to forget that Christian priests, ministers and lay people protesting the Nazis were murdered along with politicians, Gypsies, homosexuals, and the mentally and physically handicapped.

The industry urges the movies and television to depict the horrors of camp life under the guise of educating people about those events. The media use violence and horror and murder and mayhem to make money, because they know the American people are entertained by it. Thus the horrors of the holocaust become trivialized along with the death and torture of human beings in the violent American media. We are no longer horrified by horror.

Schindler's List and *The Pianist* depict violence, murder and death under the guise of heroism under adversity. These are artistic moneymakers, because they entertain us with terror and violence. They, too, lead to the trivialization of human suffering. One can call these films art, but, more deeply, they are entertainment for profit.

I know many people who are afraid to criticize the policies of the Israeli government, because they fear being called anti-Semites. This connection is fostered by the holocaust industry's insistence that the horror of the Holocaust excuses any criticism of Israel. My fearful friends need to learn to be bold.

The excesses of the Holocaust presentations make many Americans accuse the mass media being controlled by Jews. Anti-Semites need very little excuse to vent their deepest prejudices. My own view is the mass media does what makes money, whether it is controlled by Jews or Gentiles makes very little difference.

Yes, we need to be reminded and educated about the horror of the holocaust. I fear the effect of this overkill, exploiting the holocaust, makes many turn away from these horrible events. The reaction of people may be like mine when watching television. When the commercials come on, I don't pay attention. When I see something about the Holocaust, I ignore it.

We do need to pay attention to events from the Holocaust years—those that need genuine reparation and justice, such as the insurance claim of Ramon Rakover. But the repetition and exploitation of the Holocaust, instead of educating, trivializes it.

On the Israeli – Palestinian Situation 11/14/09

One friend says, "The Palestinians are not all good and the Jews are not all bad." Amos Oz, says, "...the core of the Israeli-Palestinian is a clash between right and right, and often a class between wrong and wrong."[7]

Prof. Rothman at the Fromm is said something to the effect that most American Jews are not very religious but are emotionally connected to Israel; it is hard for them to be objective about the Palestinian's plight. Israel is an emotional and identity issue for most Jews, not a rational one.

I continue stand against the Israeli government's treatment of the Palestinians. As a follower of Jesus, I choose to stand for the poor, ill educated and persecuted against the powers and principalities. The Palestinians are the underdog, and Israel is powerful, wealthy, heavily armed and supported by the United States.

President Jimmy Carter 6/18/09

Good for President Jimmy Carter (the *San Francisco Chronicle*, June 17, 2009). He has the courage to speak the truth to power. The Israeli, Palestinian and U.S. governments listen to him. The social and political policy toward Israel is *don't ask, don't tell.* Don't ask about Israeli policies and don't tell people what you think about that country's leadership. Carter asks the tough questions and tells the truth as he sees it. Liberals must not be afraid to be called anti-Semites when we ask and tell. Jimmy Carter has no fear of being called names.

I have sent this next letter to the *Chronicle* and hope they print it.

To the Editor of the SF Chronicle:

The assertion that there is a "new anti-Semitism" (the *San Francisco Chronicle*, Saturday, January 27, 2007) is a

---

7 *Sari Nusseibeh and Amos Oz were jointly awarded the Siegfried Unseld Prize in Berlin on September 28, 2010. "A Tragic Struggle" and "The Magic Within Us" are drawn from their acceptance speeches.* http://www.nybooks.com/blogs/nyrblog/2010/oct/13/two-views-mideast-peace/

call for Jews, Christians, Muslims and everyone else to look again at the adage, "know thyself." We all need to look and observe our real and true feelings about Jews. We should ruthlessly root out the feeling of the old anti-Semitism where it lingers within us. We can be sure that we are clear about the humanity and freedom of all Jews. We can also courageously oppose the policies of the Israeli government. I, and many others, can clearly state, "I am opposed to those policies against the Palestinians" and say in the same breathe, 'I am not an anti-Semite.

Robert Warren Cromey

San Francisco, California

The Israeli Supreme court upholds the killing of suspected Palestinian militants by assassination rather than by capture and a trial. If the army can go to all the trouble to find the hideouts, send drone airplanes to pinpoint the killing of these people, why can't they arrest them and bring them to trial? Murder is easier and more convenient than adhering to international law, I suppose.

What to Do about Israel

Dear Friends,

I think an important step in bringing about peace in the Palestinian-Israeli conflict is to urge the Congress to suspend financial aid to Israel. The following allows congress people to vote for aid to Israel then vote for an amendment to make aid conditional on an end to the occupation. Joe Biden is chair of the Senate Foreign Relations Committee. Rabbi Michael Lerner added wisdom to this proposal. If you are willing to sign this, email it back to me. I will collect the signatures and snail mail them to the Senate. We could all send similar letters to our own Senators and to the Prez.

Robert

We the undersigned urge the U.S. Congress to cut severely the three-billion-dollar aid to Israel. This amount is one fourth of the whole foreign aid budget. Some aid could resume when Israel ends its occupation of Palestinian lands.

Robert Warren Cromey, Rector
Trinity Episcopal Church
San Francisco, California

A letter to my Senators:

Dear Senators Feinstein and Boxer,

I am writing you to urge you *not* to support the proposed Feinstein-McConnell amendment to the Senate version of the Foreign Operations Appropriations Bill for FY2002. The Feinstein-McConnell amendment would sanction the Palestinian people, including the possibility of ending U.S. economic assistance if the President finds that the Palestine Liberation Organization (PLO) or the Palestinian Authority (PA) did not fulfill a commitment made during the Oslo-era peace process.

Since the September 2000 outbreak of the Palestinian uprising against Israel's brutal military occupation, members of Congress have introduced a slew of blatantly one-sided, anti-Palestinian resolutions that blame the victims of this occupation (the Palestinians) for the plight inflicted on them by the occupying power (Israel). Not only do these bills place the blame for the breakdown of the peace process solely on Palestinian shoulders, they also tend to be wholly uncritical of illegal Israeli actions (extra-judicial killings of Palestinian activists, bombings of Palestinian civilian targets with U.S. supplied weaponry, the demolition of Palestinian homes, destruction of Palestinian infrastructure, and more) that characterize Israel's attempt to suppress this uprising.

Such one-sided resolutions, in addition to severely distorting the terms of reference of the Israel-Palestine conflict by ignoring Israel's brutal military occupation, are irresponsible. They place Congress squarely on the side of the Jewish *pro-occupation* camp and inimically opposed to the Jewish, Arab and Muslim *pro-just peace camp*. They completely de-legitimize any U.S. efforts to serve as an *honest broker* to the conflict and align U.S. policy unflinchingly with Israel's repressive military occupation. They help to stoke anti-American sentiments among Palestinians in particular and Arabs in general by demonstrating that no matter how many Palestinians Israel kills, Congress will always congratulate Israel and condemn Palestinians. In turn, anti-American sentiments rebound to harm U.S. national security interests by serving as fodder for organizations that carry out terrorist acts designed to kill Americans (e.g., the U.S.S. Cole bombing in Yemen).

The Feinstein-McConnell amendment is a particularly egregious example of these one-sided resolutions. It tasks the President to deliver a report to the relevant Congressional committees on the compliance of the PLO and PA with the Oslo-era commitments that it made yet there is no provision for the President to report on the compliance of Israel with its commitments. If the President finds that either the PLO or the PA has not complied with its commitments then the President must apply one or more of the following sanctions: 1) deny visas to PLO and PA officials; 2) downgrade the status of PLO offices in the United States; 3) designate the PLO as a terrorist organization; 4) prohibit U.S. foreign assistance to the West Bank and Gaza Strip. Yet the amendment contains no provisions that would sanction Israel if it does not comply with its commitments.

Israel has made numerous Oslo-era commitments that it has failed to fulfill and, in the process, has violated in letter or in spirit the agreements that it signed with the PLO. For instance, Israel has doubled the number of settlers living in illegal settlements on Palestinian occupied territories since the beginning of the Oslo process, violating its commitment not to undertake any actions that would prejudge the disposition of final status issues. Contrary to what has been signed by Israel and the PLO in internationally-binding agreements, Israel has refused to release Palestinian political prisoners, impeded the progress of construction on the Gaza seaport, shut down the Gaza International Airport and prevented the functioning of a "safe passage" between the West Bank and Gaza Strip, just to name a few of Israel's many failed commitments. Worst of all, Israel has entrenched its occupation of Palestinian territory and has not demonstrated a willingness to end this occupation and withdraw as stipulated in U.N. Security Council Resolution 242--the foundation upon which the Oslo process was constructed.

It is unacceptable and irresponsible for Congress to hold only one side to the conflict responsible for fulfilling the commitments that it made to its peace partner. Adopting the Feinstein-McConnell amendment could enshrine a blatant double standard into U.S. law. I find it offensive that Congress would even consider adopting such an uneven-handed policy at a time when the United States is attempting to act as an "honest broker" to the Israel-Palestine conflict, implementing the Mitchell Commission recommendations (which call on both sides to take steps to halt the violence and resume political negotiations), and bringing the parties closer to achieving a just, comprehensive and lasting peace.

Sincerely,

Robert Warren Cromey

San Francisco, CA 94114

A Palestinian Martin Luther King Jr.

The brutality of the Israeli soldiers and the violence of the Palestinian resistance will keep on getting worse and going nowhere. Neither side has shown much good faith in working out the details of various agreements to bring about peace in that Holy Land. Rabbi Michael Lerner editor of *Tikkun* magazine has suggested an action designed to shame the Israel military and bring justice to the Palestinians. He calls for a peaceful nonviolent movement in the style of Martin Luther King, Jr., Mohandas K. Gandhi and Nelson Mandela.

King brought down the legal barriers to integration and freedom for African Americans by showing the world the vicious brutality of Southern peace officers at Selma and Montgomery, Alabama. Peaceful marchers and demonstrators were attacked, hosed down, beaten and spit upon by white American citizens and police, whose exploits were shown to the nation and world by television cameras. The injustice of racial segregation humiliated the majority of the citizens of the United States.

Gandhi brought an end to British cruelty and inhuman treatment of Indians by peaceful, disciplined, direct nonviolent demonstrations. The British were shamed into letting the people of India go.

This kind of organizing is where big business could really help. Grants to community organizing agencies are needed to finance training in nonviolence. If our moguls are willing to shell out money for weapons, they might consider money to organize for nonviolence training among Palestinians. Political and violent means have failed to bring peace. Peaceful nonviolence could do the job.

Robert Warren Cromey

Rector, Trinity Episcopal Church,

San Francisco, CA

Pains and Friendship

Here is a bit of an email dialogue between a very old and dear Jewish friend and me. We met in September 1949. It depicts the sharp differences friends can have and remain friends. Neither of us will ever change our positions. I am not fond of these discussions and have agreed out loud with some friends and tacitly with others not to make this painful issue part of our discussions.

I will call my friend Israel. He sent me the following story in response to my negative view of Prime Minister Netanyahu's recent visit to the United States

Israel - Short Story

Dr. Arieh Eldad was instrumental in establishing the Israeli National Skin Bank, which is the largest in the world. The National Skin Bank stores skin for every day needs as well as for wartime or mass casualty situations.

This skin bank is hosted at the *Hadassah Ein Kerem* University hospital in Jerusalem where I was the Chairman of plastic surgery. This is how I was asked to supply skin for an Arab woman from Gaza , who was hospitalized in Soroka Hospital in Beersheva after her family burned her. Usually, such atrocities happen among Arab families when the women are suspected of having an affair.

We supplied all the needed homografts for her treatment. She was successfully treated by my friend and colleague, Prof. Lior Rosenberg and discharged to return to Gaza. She was invited for regular follow-up visits to the outpatient clinic in Beersheva.

One day she was caught at a border crossing wearing a suicide belt. She meant to explode herself in the outpatient clinic of the hospital where they saved her life. It seems that her family promised her that if she did that they would forgive her.

This is only one example of the war between Jews and Muslims in the Land of Israel. It is not a territorial conflict. This is a civilization conflict, or rather a war between civilization & barbarism.

Robert. I have no doubt believing this story is true. I try not to argue from the particular to the general. I ask what are the causes for such rage?

Israel. Just want to clarify your response. Are you referring to the rage exhibited by parents attempting to burn their daughter to death, or the rage of a family wishing to kill innocent people who saved their daughter's life and made her whole again?

Robert. I ask what are the causes of such rage that a Palestinian would want to become a human bomb killing innocent people in Israel?

Israel. Robert, dear friend, thank you for your response. Your answer now confirms what I have suspected for a long time. You have chosen to blind yourself to reality and attempt to justify your positions on moral issues by cherry picking from the teachings of Jesus that best suit your intellectual and emotional bent. For starters, just look at the obvious contradictions in the following. Enough material there for a month of sermons.

In Matthew 5:17, Jesus says:

Do not think that I have come to abolish the Law or the Prophets; I have not come to abolish them, but to fulfill them."

In Matthew 5:38-39, Jesus says:

"You have heard that it was said, 'eye for eye, and tooth for tooth.' But I tell you, do not resist an evil person. If someone strikes you on the right cheek, turn to him the other also."

In Matthew 5:28-30, Jesus says:

"But I tell you that anyone who looks at a woman lustfully has already committed adultery with her in his heart. If your right eye causes you to sin, gouge it out and throw it away. It is better for you to lose one part of your body than for your whole body to be thrown into hell. And if your right hand causes you to sin, cut it off and throw it away. It is better for you to lose one part of your body than for your whole body to go into hell.

In Mark 10:25, Jesus says:

It is easier for a camel to go through the eye of a needle than for a rich man to enter the Kingdom of God.

Robert. I did not say that I agreed with the Palestinian or any individual or group's notion of suicide bombing. Of course I think it is an awful and terrible thing. Thank you for the lesson in scripture. I reiterate, I ask what are the causes of such rage that a Palestinian would want to become a human bomb killing innocent people in Israel?

Israel. Robert, when you find the answer to why Muslim suicide bombers kill other Muslims almost every day then you will have the answer to your question. Clue: check out the Koran.

Robert: The Koran, like the Hebrew Bible and the New Testament, was written by many hands over many generations by people with various historical and ethical beliefs. I do not take the Koran literally any more than I take the Bible literally. Thoughtful Muslims do not either. Many Muslims, Christians and Jews are literalists and fundamentalists and pick and choose what they take literally.

Oppressed and frustrated people will always express themselves in violence. I am sad and sorry to note that. Some suicide bombers are a result of the policies of the Israeli government.

I think the Israeli government's treatment of the Palestinians has been horrific. Camps, poverty, degrading their values and traditions, military brutality, breaking agreements, walls, building on disputed property, harassing free movement, blockades, constant hindering negotiations and disregarding United Nation's mandates all stand in the way of peace and tranquility in Israel. Fifty years of that policy has resulted in that rage, anger and radical desire for revenge. I do not condone it. That is what I see the root causes of suicide bombers to be.

I end this dialogue, not because Israel has nothing more to say or that I won. Nobody wins. But it is an example of how loving friends can be friends and disagree. Thank you, Israel.

Some Thoughts about Israel, Iran and the Church

- What Netanyahu wants, the American Public Affair Committee wants. What the APAC wants is what our politicians want. Our politicians want the support and money of the wealthy Jews who have the power to sway elections.

Senator Mitch McConnell (Kentucky) wants the United States to use overwhelming military force against Iran if American intelligence shows that Teheran decides to build nuclear weapons or enrich uranium. Remember when American intelligence said Iraq was building nuclear weapons? We invaded, destroyed that country, and killed hundreds of thousands of civilians. American casualties were five thousand dead and 30,000 wounded. Our government has pledged to rebuild Iraq at taxpayer's expense.

Violence begets violence. Overwhelming military force against Iran has unforeseeable consequences that will kill people and destroy nations and bring division among and hate against all concerned.

• The American Affairs Committee and Benjamin Netanyahu are pressing President Obama into preparing for war against Iran if that country develops nuclear weapons. The President is insisting wisely on letting policies of sanctions and isolation to get the government of Iran to cease its actions.

The outrage of the government and the people of Iran, a sovereign nation, is quite understandable. They don't want others interfering in their internal policies. This is especially galling to Iran, as Israel is widely believed to possess nuclear weapons. The U.S has not pressed that country about its nuclear capability. The United States, Russia, the United Kingdom, France, India, Pakistan and North Korea all possess nuclear weapons. Frankly, Iran is no more a threat to using nuclear weapons than any of the others. They are smart people who know what war destroys.

War brings death and injury not so much to the military but the civilians, the elderly, women and children Violence begets violence. It looks like we learn nothing from the last ten years of war.

- Here is Wikipedia on Nuclear Weapons:

Since the bombings of Hiroshima and Nagasaki, nuclear weapons have been detonated on over two thousand occasions for testing purposes and demonstrations. Only a few nations possess such weapons or are suspected of seeking them. The only countries known to have detonated nuclear weapons — and that acknowledge possessing such weapons — are (chronologically by date of first test) the United States, the Soviet Union (succeeded as a nuclear power by Russia), the United Kingdom, France, the People's Republic of China, India, Pakistan, and North Korea. In addition, Israel is also widely believed to possess nuclear weapons, though it does not acknowledge having them.[4][5] [6] One state, South Africa, has admitted to having previous fabricated nuclear weapons in the past, but has since disassembled their arsenal and submitted to international safeguards.[7][8]

If the US goes to war to defend Israel, I believe the undercurrents of anti-Semitism alive and sick in this country will erupt. I suspect this will be true among Southerners, black and white, poor, bikers, neo-Nazi and extreme, right-wing white supremacists. It will be taken out on Jewish business people, especially violence against Jews who are alone and isolated. I also believe there is plenty of anti-Semitism among the genteel WASPs and upper-crust Roman Catholics. I hope I am wrong. I truly do. But I have a lurking fear.

I suspect my own motives in this, as genteel anti-Semitism was part of my family upbringing. My long

---

8 http://en.wikipedia.org/wiki/Nuclear_weapon See article for notes.

time criticism of the Israeli government's treatment of the Palestinians may color my judgment. But I know I am not an anti-Semite. I have been accused of being one by some of my critics. But my Jewish friends remain friends knowing quite clearly of my criticism of the Israeli government and APAC.

We must not let the fear of being judged an anti-Semite prevent us from criticizing Israeli policies that have lead to oppression of the Palestinians and to the threat of war. We cannot be intimidated by such fears. If we lose friends who don't want to listen to our views, what have we lost?

Since the leadership in Iran is clearly anti-Semitic and denies the holocaust, it is no wonder that many in Israel and the United States fear Iran. While that fear is real, it should not direct American foreign policy that involves the whole Mid-East and not just Israel. President Obama has made himself clear on that, and we should support him.

American politicians want money and support from American Jews. It is no wonder that thoughtful, objective evaluation by the administration and congress of Israel-Iran relations is always pro-Israel. We saw the ludicrous support Netanyahu received when he spoke to the joint session of Congress last year.

Here is a role that American Christians can provide leadership and a more objective voice in the beating war drums in Israel and Washington, DC. I don't mean General Conventions and Assemblies of various denominations. I mean local parish churches need to deal with this dangerous issue. Clergy and lay people on local levels can take antiwar stands on this issue. They can provide discussion and

communication between Jews, Muslims and themselves.

Another war in the mid-east where the United States
is not threatened on our soil is useless and can only
bring more dissension and violence — mostly to the
innocent people of Iran, Israel and other countries,
too.

Negotiations

Here is the *New Yorker's* Hendrick Hertzberg's quotation of
Netanyahu's demands in dealing with the Palestinians. (June
6, 2011 issue)

> …recognition of Israel as Jewish state as a precondition;
> no negotiations with a Palestinian political entity in
> which Hamas is represented; no Palestinian refugees,
> no matter how few or how symbolic, to be admitted to
> Israel; indefinite Israeli military control of the Jordan
> River; an undivided Jerusalem as 'the United capital of
> Israel,' no part of which presumably would be available
> to be the capital of Palestine.

Is it any wonder the Palestinian leaders and people do not
want to negotiate? These are all the items that should be on the
table for discussion. Israel proclaims itself the only democracy
in the Middle East, yet denies negotiations with a popularly
elected Hamas.

How can Palestinians learn to accept Israel, which will
not even discuss the issue of *recognition of Israel*. Discussion,
dialogue, education are ways to create change of hearts and
minds. Discussion of refugees after fifty years of camps and
military control must be part of the negotiations. Not to
allow discussion of the sacred city of Jerusalem as a home to
Palestinians fails to understand the power of symbolism and
religion in the hearts of Palestinians.

Because the Prime Minister has support from his cabinet
and much of his government and the U.S. government, there

can only be pain, suffering and more bloodshed on the parts of both sides.

May 26, 2011, Response to Netanyahu's Visit

The Honorable Nancy Pelosi, Dianne Feinstein and Barbara Boxer,

In Israel's Prime Minister Netanyahu's visit to the United States he has showed utter disregard and contempt for President Obama, the United Nations, the Arab world and most of the countries of Europe. The Israeli government's treatment of the Palestinians has been horrific. Camps, military brutality, breaking agreements, walls, building on disputed property, constant hindering of negotiations and disregarding United Nation's mandates all hinder peace and tranquility in Israel.

The US Congress pandering to Netanyahu was ludicrous. I hope President Mahmoud Abbas of the Palestinian Authority will also be invited to address a joint session of Congress.

Israel's leaders have refused to negotiate with the Palestinians until they repudiate Hamas, a group democratically elected to leadership by the people. In addition Israeli leaders have indicated they would not negotiate with any group who does not believe in the right of Israel to exist.

Negotiating about those two important issues should be exactly what the discussions are all about. People of good will can sit down and deal with the hardest issues. They must not be preconditions to talking together. The refusal to do so smacks of not wanting to negotiate under any circumstances.

Lest you think I am just one more anti-Israeli-government crank, please note these web sites of Jews and others who support Palestinians.

- http://jfjfp.com/ (Jews for Justice for Palestinians)
- http://www.tikkun.org (Rabbi Michael Lerner)
- http://www.womeninblack.org/en/about (Women in Black: For Justice. Against the War.)
- http://jewishvoiceforpeace.org (Jewish Voice for Peace)

Sincerely, RWC

In an email, I copied Rabbi Lerner's quote below from an earlier letter to me.

With Israel's Prime Minister Netanyahu's visit to the United States, I have received a number of emails from friends in support of Israel. I replied to one reiterating my long held and unwavering position. Years ago I said, "I am a Palestinian.

Responses to my email about the Netanyahu visit.

- No, Mr. Netanyahu! Americans Don't Support Your Intransigence and Rejection of a Plausible Path to Peace. We stand with President Obama on Peace Negotiations. Rabbi Michael Lerner
- Here are the replies I received to my "I am a Palestinian statement."
- Robert: I stand with you—a Palestinian.
- I am with you 100 percent and have been for many years.

AMEN!
Good for you for sticking your neck out. Glad you're not a giraffe.
Well said, comrade!

- The US Congress pandering to Netanyahu was ludicrous. Yes, and very sad. I believe Israel does not want and will do everything it can to prevent the establishment of a Palestinian state.
- On this, as on so many other subjects, I am with you all the way.
- The leading and most effective anti-Zionists are Jews.
- I am heartened knowing someone besides myself isn't in lockstep with the Israeli party line that has captured and imperiled the US for a very long time.

Here is the last letter I received from Jewish Voice for Peace....
Here is their website, <info@jewishvoiceforpeace.org>

Both sides seem to have very stiff necks, but Israel's is stiffer. And as long as that continues, there'll be no resolution. Hopefully, though, the people/individuals themselves will keep trying to meet face-to-face and get to know each other as human beings.

You have a noble position and it need repeating again and again.

Here is the only negative:

Well, you are entitled to your opinion. I think you are way off base.

Returning Gaza accomplished nothing except more rockets.

I completely agree with Netanyahu when he asked, "would you live with that?". By the way, would you?

And I would never negotiate with anyone who is dedicated to my destruction.

What would happen to Israel if the Palestinians had military superiority? There would be no negotiations.

I am sure there were other negative responses, but I did not get them. I was particularly delighted with so many positive emails. The people opposed to Israeli policies and the United States pandering to the Israeli government are not as public as those who support them.